Praise for *The Buy Right Approach to Property Investing*

Trust is a big thing when you are spending money, especially hundreds of thousands of dollars, or even more. You would have to go a long way to find more trustworthy people than Cate and Pete. They are also smart, understand the theory behind successful property investment and, very importantly, personally invest in property themselves.

Too many property spruikers write about making a quick buck in property because it sounds exciting and sexy. The reality is as Cate and Pete point out: you need to be cautious, calculated and patient so that you end up buying the right property in the right location. If you can do this, you will make money in property, slowly but surely.

I am sure that you will enjoy reading this book as it has countless tips on what to do right and also what not to do.
Peter Koulizos, property lecturer

I have had the privilege of knowing and working with Cate and Pete in different ways over the years and have long considered them two of the very best in the property investment business. Now, they have combined their decades of experience and knowledge, somehow in just one book! Their book should be on the must-read list of every aspiring property investor. By following Cate and Pete's simple, yet powerful, property investment approach, it is possible to build a portfolio that will ride out the peaks and troughs of property market seasons, so you can financially thrive and genuinely change the course of your life.
Nicola McDougall, Chair, Property Investment Professionals of Australia

I've known Cate Bakos and Pete Wargent for many years; both are exceptional professionals in their respective fields. As a former president of REBAA, Cate has demonstrated her commitment to ethical business practices and client care, providing invaluable insights and guidance to help clients navigate the property market with confidence through both good and bad economic environments. And whether it's macro or microeconomic aspects of real estate, Pete's deep understanding of local real estate markets, coupled with his down-to-earth nature and his ability to dissect complex data and translate it into understandable insights, makes him a trusted resource for anyone seeking reliable information and advice.

Together, Cate and Pete have co-authored a book that promises to be a valuable resource for anyone interested in navigating Australia's real estate market. With their combined expertise and dedication to excellence, it's a must read!
Catherine Cashmore, Director of Cashmore & Co Real Estate, President of Prosper Australia and Editor of *Catherine Ca~~·········~~ *~~L····~~ *~~Cycle Investor~~

T0359711

THE
BUY RIGHT
APPROACH TO
PROPERTY
INVESTING

Mastering
the skills to
invest wisely
in property

CATE BAKOS & PETE WARGENT

MAJOR
STREET

MAJOR
STREET

First published in 2024 by Major Street Publishing Pty Ltd
info@majorstreet.com.au | majorstreet.com.au

NATIONAL
LIBRARY
OF AUSTRALIA

A catalogue record for this book is available
from the National Library of Australia

Printed book ISBN: 978-1-923186-09-5
Ebook ISBN: 978-1-923186-10-1

Cover design by Typography Studio
Internal design by Production Works
Printed in Australia by Griffin Press

10 9 8 7 6 5 4 3 2 1

Contents

Welcome to the Buy Right Approach

The world is changing, and advances in technology mean that it's changing faster than ever before. Naturally, this brings challenges, but it also offers opportunities to the well-prepared.

As real-estate professionals and top industry experts here in Australia, we have decades of investing experience. Despite the media noise about catastrophic housing market collapses, we both believe that property will remain the vehicle which affords most aspirational Aussies the opportunity to get ahead and design the lifestyle they want to enjoy.

Over the years there have been many gloomy predictions about the future of property as an asset class. What we've learned, though, is that there are market cycles: winter seasons are followed by summer seasons. Over the long term, if you stick to the fundamentals and focus on well-located properties, the results can be outstanding.

 Hello! I'm Cate

I'm a fully licensed real estate agent, a Property Investment Professionals of Australia (PIPA) Qualified Property Investment Adviser® and a qualified mortgage broker. I've been active in property purchasing and investing for 28 years now – over half my life.

Hi, I'm Pete

I'm a chartered accountant with a range of professional qualifications in finance and real estate and have been an avid property investor for two decades, both in Australia and overseas. I'm also the author of six previous books on property, investing, and personal finance. I have a passion for continual learning and improvement, and am always keen to share my lessons and insights with as many people as possible!

Our experience has led us to believe three things:

1. Smart property decisions can genuinely change the course of your life. They changed ours – and we've seen the same thing play out for hundreds (if not thousands) of clients and friends.
2. Property investing is something that you can be better than average at with just a bit of strategic thinking and good information. Buy right in property and you can really thrive.
3. Property is a forgiving asset class. Even if you purchase a property that, on reflection, is only a 6/10 in terms of quality, time does heal. Time *in* the market – time owning an investment, in other words – makes a huge difference to an investor's long-term wealth.

Of course, we're here to help you to achieve better results: to buy right every time, and to accelerate your journey to property success with fewer setbacks. Still, the most important thing to know about property investing is that it's a long-term game and requires long-term thinking, long-term decisions, and the ability to ignore media hype. People overestimate what they can achieve in a year or two but hugely underestimate what they can achieve in a decade plus. Sticking to the strategy is essential: those who have a clear plan but deviate from it for short-term reasons regret it later on!

What exactly will *The Buy Right Approach to Property Investing* teach you? Stick around and you'll discover our recipe for property wealth and success, founded on our real-world experience as property professionals.

Our Buy Right Approach is defined by cautious optimism: cautious because you need to make sensible decisions and manage debt carefully; optimistic because over the long term, the size and wealth of the Aussie population and economy is going to grow dramatically and push up property prices in desirable areas. In this book we share trade secrets on how and where to buy in order to build a powerhouse property portfolio which will future-proof your wealth and deliver consistent results for you over the years and decades to come.

Right, let's get into it.

1

Who are we?

This book shares the lessons we've learned and the knowledge we've gained over decades of real-life experience in property investing and supporting clients on their property journeys. One of the things we've learned is that a foundation of successful property investing is understanding and working with (or around!) your specific personality – your strengths and weaknesses. So, let's take a look, here at the start of the book, at our personal stories, our personalities, and our investing history and credentials. Like everyone else, we've endured our share of ups and downs, but a few good decisions have delivered us huge benefits over time.

We met one another through the property industry, by the way – we'd admired each other's writing and commentary, and a friendship grew pretty organically. These days, we do a fair amount of collaboration: as well as writing this book together, we never let distance get in the way of a good podcast recording or webinar, and Budget Night live sessions on LinkedIn have become an annual tradition.

 **Cate's story**

When I was growing up, I expected that I'd do something 'professional' as a career.

I'm the eldest child of three; for some years, I was the eldest of five, when my parents took in my two cousins following a tragic accident. I grew up on Victoria's Mornington Peninsula before it was the cool, rich holiday-magnet that it is today.

We had bunk beds and all the hustle and bustle that a big, busy household creates. My parents worked hard, and our family business – a hi-fi shop – was a stark reminder of the life that a business owner could expect. My dad came home around 8 p.m. every night, and my mum ran a tight ship with her domestic duties woven around her part-time nursing career.

My parents didn't go to university, and the bright, shining lights of Melbourne didn't attract them, but city life was always my goal. Have you seen the movie *Muriel's Wedding*, about the girl who wanted to leave Porpoise Spit and make it in the city? Well, that was me!

My parents expected we'd all go to university: they'd provisioned for us to focus on our schooling and promoted discipline in our studies. I think it was because they knew it offered a more stable future, perhaps free from late nights and long hours in a commercial or self-employed role. My dad had high hopes for me, and studying medicine was a common discussion topic. But truth be told, I'd have been a terrible doctor. I don't cope with blood and lacerations, and I don't particularly like dealing with death either.

Nonetheless, back in 1992 I aimed for a medical degree – and landed in a science degree at Monash University. I never deliberately chose to pursue chemistry, but it was the discipline I fell into. I felt like a driver on the Tullamarine Freeway: I'd gotten on, and I couldn't get off.

When I finished my degree, I was ready to take an exit ramp into the working world but was offered the opportunity to stay on another year in the lab and write an honours thesis. I remember casually telling my dad that I had been offered an honours place but wouldn't be taking it up. After all, I'd embarked on the science degree in the hope I could transition into Monash medicine, but chemistry was a far cry from general practice. My dad encouraged me to do the honours year, though, and so I did. I finished in 1993 and got a job at Orica, a global chemical giant. I was not to become a doctor after all.

I enjoyed my role at Orica for three years when my boss at the time, a lovely guy called Alan, encouraged me to consider a sales and marketing role within the company group. I was terrified by the concept, as I was fairly shy, but I took on the challenge nonetheless, moving to a subsidiary company, Dulux. In 2003, I won their Marketing Professional of the Year award, which came with a cash bursary and a gold watch.

I then made the bold leap into real estate and started working as a young sales agent in a bayside firm in Melbourne. My parents were concerned and wondered why I'd thrown away a great corporate job with a company car and salary for a commission-only role, but my burning desire to follow my heart couldn't be reasoned with!

After my first year at Hodges Real Estate, I won their Rising Star award. I didn't stay in property sales, however. As much as I loved the people interaction and the thrill of the deal, I knew something was missing. I particularly wanted more of a strategic and consultative role, identifying quality property and analysing market trends. So, when I was pregnant with my daughter, I took the opportunity to complete my Certificate IV in Mortgage Broking, and in 2006, with a newborn at home, commenced a new role as a mortgage broker. I learnt so much about everything from loan products to bank policy, construction lending to cashflow analysis. It was a challenging time, with the Global Financial Crisis striking in 2008, but to this day I consider it one of the most valuable apprenticeships I could have served.

My love of giving property advice was what compelled me to return to real estate. I enrolled at Swinburne University to complete my Certificate IV in Property Services so that I could get my full real estate agent's licence. However, by chance I was introduced to a young business in North Melbourne called Empower Wealth that was looking for a senior mortgage broker. When I shared my burning ambitions regarding real estate, I was offered an opportunity to join as a director and head up a property services arm to the business. It was the longest job interview I've ever had, but it was a great role. My colleagues supported me, and the personal growth was exciting. I was a Telstra Business Awards finalist, and I won the YIP Top Buyer's Agent award in 2013.

In 2014, I left Empower Wealth and launched my own property-buying business, Cate Bakos Property. It was a difficult decision, but the company I'd worked for was expanding fast and I sensed the boutique nature I had loved was changing. I didn't wish to buy interstate (and I still don't). Our visions weren't aligned anymore; it was time to shine on my own.

It was a bold move. I recall the lease I took on, the photocopier I signed up for, the staff I employed and the signage I ordered, all in one week. I thought to myself, 'I really hope this works'. Thankfully, it did!

There are some interesting parallels between being a buyer's agent and my original ambition of being a doctor in general practice. One day I was chatting with a client about my career switch, and they quizzed me as to how it all came about. I talked about the things I enjoy about my work, of which there are many: the randomness of each day; the hectic pace that some days throw at me; the things that are beyond my control and how I adapt; the discipline it takes to keep moving at pace when required; the way I like to deal with challenges; supporting people through upset; looking at every unique case and planning a suitable pathway forward; having the difficult discussions with people; maintaining an acute attention to detail; celebrating the exciting wins; and of course, managing high-stakes outcomes that are often highly emotional for clients.

I realised that many of these things had been aspects of general practice that I thought I'd enjoy, which are very much alive and kicking in my buyer's agency business, with the addition of some fabulous moments of commercial grit.

Investing solo and as a couple

I've bought and sold property from a young age. My first contract was signed at age 21, when I was still working part-time in a supermarket deli at night, and saving at a rapid pace thanks to the attractive penalty rates. I supplemented my income by tutoring maths through my undergraduate years, and then my honours-year lab-demonstrator role paid handsomely for someone who was used to supermarket wages.

I managed to save a 40 per cent deposit, which was no mean feat for a 21-year-old. Within five years I had upgraded to my third home with my high-school boyfriend, who by then was my husband. We made many of the classic rookie investing errors during these five years, from listening to the wrong people to financial literacy blunders.

Our most critical mistake, however, related to our mismatched appetites for renovation, investing, and building wealth. I must have seemed so exhausting to him; my desire to build wealth and give myself options in life was burning fiercely. This was my first big lesson on the huge impact individual personality has on investing.

Fast-forwarding a few more years, when I embarked on my career in real estate with Hodges in 2003, I was a single woman again. I pressed the restart button on my home life and purchased a glorious little north-facing 1960s apartment by the beach in Mentone. The mortgage on this was tame, and I had comfortable buffers in my offset account to enable me to give the career move every chance of success.

Melbourne real estate was performing well, and my personal house sales netted some good profits. I don't attribute the gains we made solely to Melbourne's growth, though: I'd picked two exciting growth areas that I'd earmarked as candidates for immediate gentrification. There was no study and no analysis: just a keen sense of demographic change in two areas neighbouring trendy suburbs. (We look at gentrification in more detail in chapter 4.)

My goal of attaining financial freedom came a lot closer to reality when I met my now husband, Ian. Some couples love travel, others love collecting, some love dining... the list is plentiful. Ian and I certainly share a love of travel and the outdoors, but the immediate thing I recognised was our financial alignment. Being on the same financial page as your partner is not as easy as some may think, but if the match is right, combining your natural strengths can make it feel like you have superpowers.

My husband has a natural aversion to risk and debt, and I'm sure I was a challenging partner for him in the early days of our relationship. I'm far more comfortable with risk, and for me back then, the 'right time' for the next acquisition was always as soon as it was physically possible. We smile about how our yin and yang complement each other, but the truth is, I must have given him some sleepless nights. As people grow together, though, they often wear the edges off each other, and approaches and views that initially differed can begin to align. I no longer take the financial risks I used to, nor does Ian ask for a documented strategic plan whenever I propose an idea.

Our goal was to reach financial freedom by the ages of 50 and 60 respectively – there's a decade between us, as his 1970s playlist often reminds me! Our version of financial freedom wasn't about stopping work, however, but about finding work we love. For me, that's been achieved by owning and running my own business as a buyer's agent.

I love it, even though it's often very demanding. Clients generally make critical property-purchase decisions out of hours. Saturdays are big days with open homes and auctions. The hours can be long, phone calls are non-stop, deadlines are unforgiving and often spring from nowhere, and I have to wear a number of hats as a small business owner – from HR to marketing, writing blogs to training staff. It's a very busy career and, as I've said to anyone who toys with the idea of becoming a buyer's agent, 'It's a lifestyle'.

Taking a long-term focus

I've found that financial freedom sneaks up on you once your assets are in place and your strategy is firm. My approach with property investing has been to 'buy and hold' – running my business, using my income to buy property and paying it off as quickly as I could, with the aim of living off the rent in retirement. My husband and I plotted out a careful acquisition plan, factoring in cashflows, borrowing capacity, duties, taxes, and of course, time. My years as a mortgage broker certainly aided in this planning! We also have superannuation – our fund holds two of our properties – and invest in shares to cover all the bases.

Something Pete and I have in common is that we don't want to sell our properties. When my husband and I retire, we'll sell the few properties that are interstate and likely to require serious maintenance or renovation, but the vast majority will remain in our portfolio forever (or at least, for our lifetime). And to date, we've only sold properties that gave us personal grief: we tired of the phone ringing on a Saturday night with police callouts or complaints from neighbours and property managers! I think the measure of a good portfolio is whether it's well-planned and puts limited maintenance pressure on the owner.

This is different to some approaches with which I help clients. Most people go into property investment with the goal of capital growth in mind. They may not think through in detail their debt-retirement strategy (that is, how to pay off their mortgages and other loan facilities), and many leave it to their financial planner. Upon retirement, most choose to 'divest' (sell their properties), pay the capital gains tax and find a way to reinvest the profits in a more liquid form such as shares. By this stage they're 60-somethings and the common dinner-party conversation topics are superannuation, tax deductions and entities.

My husband and I worked from conservative projections, and we had sensible buffers (mostly) in place. In the early days I threw every cent of savings into deposits; by the time the plan was in place, our buffers enabled us to sit through difficult times, vacancy periods, hefty maintenance bills and the like.

I'm 50 this year (2024), and we're no longer acquiring property. Not only have we achieved our goal of financial freedom, we've blown far past our original targets. 'Buy and hold' has a nice ring to it, but when it's done well – when you Buy Right – the results can truly be startling! Our properties are delivering a rental return that eclipses the costs associated with holding them, most of our debt has been paid down, and our current cashflow is greater than my corporate salary was. Once all our debt is paid down, this cashflow should increase substantially.

I would say, in fact, that in our quest to build our portfolio quickly, we were overly aggressive. Had we worked off less conservative figures, we may not have had to take on as much debt and carry as much risk – and we could have enjoyed our lifestyle and holiday plans at an earlier date.

As I write this book with Pete, I marvel at the different paths he and I have taken to arrive at the Buy Right Approach to investing. Best of all, we've carved our own journeys in the world of work. I doubt I could ever return to a life in corporate, and nor would I want to. The cut and thrust of running a business and a successful property portfolio is what keeps me happily busy every day. It's not the only thing that fills my cup, but it certainly helps me to enjoy the other important things in life.

My next challenge relates to helping my daughter find her way. Gifting her things is not in the plan, but inspiring her and teaching her certainly is. I enjoyed my own journey so much, and I want that for my daughter: for her to walk her own path and build her own success.

 **Pete's story**

I was born in Sheffield, England. I won't go into detail about my younger years – if you're interested in my full story, it's covered in my first book, *Get a Financial Grip*. My parents met at university in Sheffield, and while it was never forced upon us, it was assumed that my brothers and I would most likely go on to higher education – and so we did. Like many people who don't really know what they want to do in life, I decided to get a professional qualification. I think there was a kind of implied expectation that I would enter a profession (as a doctor, lawyer, accountant, or similar).

Anyway, in the absence of any better ideas – or indeed much thought – I trained to become a chartered accountant. Accountancy provides a great grounding for anyone interested in business and can open many doors, perhaps even allowing you to later become a CFO or CEO in an industry you're passionate about. I quite like working with numbers and I enjoyed parts of my professional career, but I didn't enjoy the long hours, office politics or being stuck at a desk. I felt like the free-spirited Patrick Swayze character, Bodhi, in the surfing movie *Point Break*: 'I can't live in a cage, man!'

Over time, career disillusionment combined with a change of jobs, country and relationship led to something of a quarter-life crisis for me. I just wasn't enjoying life as much as I wanted to be and found it hard to envisage myself still grafting away as an accountant in the decades to come. Evidently, I was searching for something 'more'. This search for some excitement in my life largely manifested itself in binge-drinking and partying, until eventually I realised that I had to make some wholesale changes.

When I was growing up, as I mentioned, it was probably expected that I'd have a career as a professional – not as an entrepreneur and an author, or working in real estate. Regardless, that's how it worked out, and it's suited me perfectly. I never feel like it's a chore to write a book, record a podcast, or provide TV and radio commentary on what's happening in the economy or housing market. It's all reading and research I would be doing anyway, as I'm fascinated by demographics, how people live, and watching cities and industries evolve.

Better still, I don't have sit in an office for 40 or more hours per week to do it. These days I live near the beach in Noosa, and head down for a swim whenever I feel like it. I'd find it hard (if not impossible!) to go back to an office-based role now. It's often said that you should follow your passion. If you find something you love doing, you'll never work a day in your life, and all that. I think that's partly true. After all, if you love your work, you'll be more inclined to work harder at it, to keep learning and stick at it for longer. Inevitably, in the long run it will work in your favour.

During my professional career, a more senior colleague of mine called Rob once mentioned in passing that I was 'lazy'. Actually, in the context of the discussion, he wasn't wrong. (G'day Rob, by the way, if you're reading!) I found this a bit confusing, however. I know I'm not a lazy individual! I've written and published seven books. I've written a daily blog post for a dozen years, without fail. I once decided to train from scratch to run the Sydney marathon, and achieved it within a year. I've got endless stamina for playing golf or creating daily online content. The reality is that plain accountancy just wasn't suitable for my personality type. I'm still a registered accountant (FCA), but it's not my career.

A few years ago, my friend and previous co-author Stephen Moriarty introduced me to the concept of the Enneagram assessment and the nine different personality types. It then began to dawn on me why some people were able to sit in meetings for days at a time, seemingly without ever losing interest – and why I'd sometimes felt like an alien in the office, looking around and thinking to myself, 'Surely I can't be the only person with such a low level of enthusiasm for poring over board minutes, preparing accounts or endlessly discussing the minute details of accounting systems?'

What I've learned is that... well, people are different! Some people are detail-focused and process-driven. Some people love routine, while others can't even stand to holiday in the same location twice. Some are driven by a need for stability and security; others need new experiences and adventure.

Steve pointed out to me that I'm an Enneagram type 7, an Optimist (with some elements of a type 5, the Investigator). As a type 7, I'm optimistic, enthusiastic for new projects, love freedom and adventure, and place a high value on not having constraints or a boss constantly telling me what to do. It makes sense that I wasn't destined for an amazing career in accountancy!

I bumped into one of my old schoolteachers a few years back in Brisbane, and he mentioned that I'm the sort of person who should have always been an entrepreneur instead of following a traditional career path. Given my personality type, he may well have been right.

An Achiever personality type (type 3), on the other hand, might enjoy the cut and thrust of a high-powered corporate role, and the status associated with it. In case you were wondering, Cate is a classic type 3! She's a high achiever, driven by goals, achievements, results, and excellence. When I first mentioned this to Cate, she questioned it, but after reading up on the Enneagram personality types, she admitted, 'Damn, you nailed it!'

From stocks to property

As an investor, I was mainly interested in the stock market at first, largely because my job required me to write annual reports for companies listed on the stock exchange. It was my wife, Heather, who first got me interested in property. She and I were both higher-rate taxpayers by the age of 25 or 26, which is also when we first met, in Cambridge in the UK. Soon after that, we relocated to Sydney.

She is a bit older than me, and when we met, she'd already built a large pool of equity in her first house, which she'd bought in 1996, thanks to some smart decisions. Heather comes from a farming background and had been taught that you buy land and never sell it.

Over time, I came to realise that property was something we could do together and do well. Heather bought me a few real estate guides and books which helped to fuel my inspiration. As Cate touched on, if you have a partner, you can build a property portfolio jointly. It can bring you closer together, giving you a purpose and a project to keep building and working on for many decades. In my experience, the relationship benefits of having joint goals and working together to achieve those goals are often overlooked.

When I first got into property, I was really excited. I read the material Heather gave me plus all the other books I could. I realised this was an asset class in which I could achieve great things over time through the combination of leverage and compound growth. I was never going to be a top performer in my career, but because of the way compound growth works – the results multiply and get better and better over time – I could achieve really good results in property, providing I got educated and made some smart decisions.

About leverage and compound growth

Leverage is the ability do more with less. In the context of property investing, this typically means borrowing some of the bank's money to invest in higher-value assets. For example, you could use $50,000 as a 10 per cent deposit to invest in a property worth $500,000. This effectively magnifies the results from the investment.

Compound growth has a powerful 'snowballing' effect, which means that the results get better and better over time. For example, a property investment worth $500,000 and growing in value 10 per cent per annum would be worth $550,000 in year 1 (an increase of $50,000) and $605,000 in year 2 (an increase of $55,000). By year 10, the investment would be worth nearly $1.3 million, and would increase in value in year 10 by almost $120,000!

Due to our high incomes, Heather and I had plenty of opportunity to save deposits, and a high borrowing capacity, particularly in the pre–Global Financial Crisis years. We both rose through the ranks at one of the Big Four accounting firms, up to Director level, but neither of us wanted to work in accountancy for the next few decades. I also worked in mining for a few years as Group Financial Controller, which paid very well, and was more enjoyable than working in professional practice, but still wasn't what I wanted to do for the long term. I didn't like having to be in one place for a whole week, and the lack of personal freedom and free time was hard yakka.

So, our plan was to invest as heavily as possible while we had a high combined income and borrowing was easier, and allow time to do much of the heavy lifting after that.

The great billionaire investor Charlie Munger once said that you need to do whatever it takes to make your first US$100,000… whether that's living on cut-price chicken, walking everywhere, sharing a house, working two jobs, working overtime or weekends. Whatever it takes. Then, once you have your first significant investments compounding away, you can ease up a little bit.

Looking back, that's my story in a nutshell. My wife and I both slogged away in jobs we often found tedious or frustrating, but once we owned a few investment properties each compounding away for us, we could ease off the gas a bit, as we knew the long-term results would be great.

We bought a few properties in Sydney, in Bondi (myself), Darling Harbour (jointly), and Erskineville (jointly). We subsequently went very hard into property when prices fell during the Global Financial Crisis between 2007 and 2009, buying several properties in Sydney, and then later in Brisbane and Melbourne, as well as adding further properties to our portfolio back in the UK. Since then, we've invested in other parts of the UK, such as in Leeds and in farmland, and counter-cyclically, when we've been able to, have invested in different areas of Australia.

How it often tends to work in property is that once you've grown some equity in your first property or two, you can refinance to purchase further investments. Once the whole portfolio experiences a full cycle of capital growth, you'll have generally achieved substantial equity. But that does take time. That was basically how it worked out for us.

I didn't come from a wealthy background, and I won't get an inheritance (I'm from a large Catholic family of seven, with parents separated), but my story shows that over the course of two full property cycles, it's not unrealistic to achieve your property goals through smart investing. Just note that two full property cycles might take about 15 years in total, and with lifestyle creep and rising expectations, realistically it might take perhaps 15 to 20 years for most people to achieve their goals.

I added an extra wrinkle, however, by quitting my full-time job at the age of 33 to become an entrepreneur, which made borrowing much harder. To keep moving forward, I acquired cheaper properties spread all over the place, and commercial as well as residential real estate.

It took us a bit longer than planned, but we've achieved our property investment goals. At the time of writing, some of our properties are paid off, some are making more for us than they cost to hold, and some properties (mainly in Sydney) are still costing us money to hold. My wife and I also invest in index funds and ETFs (exchange-traded funds), and have ISAs (Individual Savings Accounts) in the UK to help the kids go to uni.

Something I have in common with Cate is that I don't sell property. Don't get me wrong, I've thought about it many times – I regularly fantasise about selling properties to go travelling, buy cars, or reinvest in other asset classes. But then I remember a few things. First, I know from my business studies about the awesome power of compound growth when you let it flourish for years and decades. As Charlie Munger said, you should never interrupt compound growth unnecessarily. We've always tried to focus on buying properties in the best locations we can, so hopefully one day we can pass them on to the kids. Second, as an accountant, I know how painful capital gains tax can be if you decide to sell.

That said, I can see us selling down some assets in retirement years. We may sell some properties to live off stock-market and fixed-income investments instead, but it partly depends on where we end up deciding to live and retire – Europe, Australia, or elsewhere.

It's worth noting that selling some of your property portfolio is quite a common strategy in retirement and can be sensible, depending on your circumstances. Due to the leverage involved in property, many investors end up 'top heavy' or heavily tilted towards real estate investments – meaning that's where most of their wealth is. So, in Australia, it's common for property investors to alter course as they approach retirement by selling some of their properties to reduce debt and/or to shift money into more cashflow-focused investments, such as commercial properties and shares. The stock market in Australia is almost tailor-made for investors seeking an income: due to the tax system, we have relatively high dividend yields, and a tax-favoured treatment for franked dividends.

There are numerous ways to tackle the retirement question, and plans can change along the way. In our experience, though, the most important thing is to grow your net worth and equity over time so that you have choices about how best to approach your retirement years.

 The takeaways

Cate and I said in our introduction to this book that property investing can change the course of your life. That's been true for both of us. That doesn't mean that you need to become a real estate agent or a property professional like we have, of course. But making smart decisions in the property market can make an enormous difference to your financial wellbeing.

You can see from our stories that Cate and I are very different people, and yet we've both had a lot of success investing in property. There is no one 'right way' to do it, although arguably there are some 'wrong ways' that generally don't work. (More on those later in the book.) If pressed, we'd say that focusing on quality over quantity is probably best, but purchasing a higher number of properties of somewhat lower quality can also work.

My business partner Andrew is a prime example of the 'quality over quantity' approach. He has a gorgeous home in a blue-chip suburb of Brisbane, and a very tidy, high-performance portfolio of high-quality houses in blue-chip suburbs of Melbourne, Brisbane, and Perth.

Mainly through necessity, I've taken a different path. As I mentioned earlier, I bought some blue-chip properties while I was employed as an accountant, but when I started my own business and borrowing became more difficult, I had to acquire cheaper properties.

In some cases, these are what I'd describe as lower-quality assets, but they were simply the best Heather and I could do at the time. The cost of this is that we deal with more property managers and there's more administration involved. You obviously want to avoid 'the assets owning you' rather than the other way around, but overall, it has worked for us. Funnily enough, some of the properties in less desirable locations have been top performers at various points in time.

I'd steer clear of the very cheapest end of the market, however, as generally there can be more problems with such properties, and the costs of fixing them can wipe out years of capital gains. Remember, it costs the same to call out a tradie whether the property is worth $200,000 or $2 million.

Your turn

Have you thought about which approach you'll use? Will you focus on owning a few quality properties, or will you acquire properties you can afford when you can afford them? Or a combination of the two?

This decision could be made for you, as it was for me, if you're self-employed or are employed on a lower income. In chapter 9 we go into how to calculate your borrowing capacity and plan your portfolio acquisitions.

This leads into another point you'll have picked up from our stories: the fact that we both still work. One of the big keys to property investing is earning enough income through employment or self-employment to save your initial deposits and buffers and then maintain a borrowing capacity. If it's at all possible, we recommend finding a career you love that pays a reasonable wage!

Charlie Munger made his observation about needing to save your first $100,000 a couple of decades ago, and the equivalent sum today might be larger – perhaps $300,000 in Aussie dollars – but the principle remains the same. If you're in your twenties and won't get a leg up from wealthy parents (we didn't) then you'll have to do whatever it takes to get started. This can be difficult, especially if you have friends, family, peers, or colleagues looking at you disapprovingly – it's interesting how people don't like their friends to take a different path. But you must do it!

If you're in your thirties, forties or beyond and also just starting out with investing, the same still applies. Maybe you're a bit further ahead: perhaps you've purchased your own home and have some equity in it, or you have savings to help you get started with investing. You'll still need surplus income to help you forge ahead with acquiring, managing, and maintaining properties, and again, finding a job or business you're passionate about is key.

Whatever age you are, though, the best time to start investing is always now. We've seen people of all ages be successful with the

Buy Right Approach! It's all about finding your own path. And, on that note, enough about us… let's talk about you!

Key points in this chapter

- Property and property decisions can literally change your life.
- There are many different ways to make money in property.
- You'll need to do whatever it takes to get started.

2

Who are you?

You've heard our stories – what about yours? What are your life goals and aspirations? Knowing what you want to get out of your Buy Right property plan is what will help you fine-tune it.

Now, how did you come to have your life goals in the first place? Considering how your goals and aspirations came to be what they are is an interesting little thought experiment.

There's an old saying: 'Give me the boy of seven, and I will show you the man'. The premise is that by the age of seven, much of our programming has been absorbed into our brains, both consciously and unconsciously. It's quite alarming when you think about it!

A British documentary series called *Up!*, which began in 1964 with its first film, *Seven Up!*, explored this concept. It followed the lives of a group of seven-year-old kids from different backgrounds, and then revisited them every seven years over the decades that followed. The good news is that the results weren't entirely predictable, which shows that you can upgrade your thinking and programming throughout your life. It was striking, however, how many of the participants have lived the kinds of lives predicted for them.

Do you ever look at the decisions made by your friends and family and wonder what on earth they're up to? It's pretty common! Life is wonderfully varied, and it takes all sorts – there are often no right or wrong answers, only the right answers for you. Let's take another look at the Enneagram model, so you can begin to think about your personality type.

As noted in the previous chapter, Cate is a type 3, a classic high Achiever, with a strong focus on goals. A natural leader, Cate likes to hit targets and attain results. This cohort tends to continue kicking goals year after year, decade after decade – Cate will likely continue working hard on her business for years to come. Oprah Winfrey is another example of a type 3: she not only became a presenter, but a successful and influential business owner with her own production company. Probably at least a third of the people who choose to read a book on real estate, like this one, will fit into this category.

By contrast, Pete is a type 7, an Optimist, more interested in adventures and experiences. He has more of a focus on freedom and flexibility and dislikes being constrained, or being told what to do by a boss. Pete also has an aversion to being tied down in one place, having previously lived not only in Sydney, Darwin, Brisbane, and Noosa, but also overseas in East Timor, Germany, and England. Ten years from now, he could easily be living in Thailand or Vietnam.

Examples of people through history who fit into this free-spirited category include the great composer Wolfgang Amadeus Mozart and consummate actor and comedian Robin Williams. You can immediately see why type 7s may have a problem with setting goals over a decade or longer, because their wants and needs are prone to change. However, a long-term 'buy and hold' focus can in fact be useful for a type 7 personality, to stop them getting too distracted by the latest fads or new ideas! To work with their personality, though, it can be easier for them to set their goals for, say, the next one, two or three years, while simultaneously having a broad, longer-term plan to keep building wealth through property.

As property advisors, we also often come across clients who are type 5s, the 'Investigator' personality type. They're in good company: Albert Einstein and Mark Zuckerberg would fit into this type. Investigators are thinkers and analysers; they tend to be quieter, more introverted, and detail-focused, and they like evidence-based investing strategies. They don't like 'noise' and prefer to take calm decisions, though they can also be prone to over-thinking or paralysis by analysis.

Without knowing anything about you personally, given that you are reading this book, it's quite probable that you are a type 3, 5, or 7, or at least have elements of those personality types. Why? Because those are the personality types which place importance on personal finances, and therefore on investing for the future. This means that it's likely you'll be driven by one or more of these sets of needs and values when it comes to money and wealth:

- Type 3 – goals, status, achievements, productivity, dislike of failure
- Type 5 – security, low risk, thoughtfulness, curiosity, independence
- Type 7 – freedom, experience, adventure, spontaneity.

Above and beyond this, you likely have sub-types which influence the way you think and plan for the future – after all, there are more than nine different types of people! Models like the Enneagram always have their limitations, too – in the end, we're all different, and we can change over time. Nevertheless, the Enneagram can be a useful framework for understanding yourself and other people, particularly in the context of setting goals.

Your turn

Take an Enneagram test – there are plenty of them available for free on the internet. It's a worthwhile exercise to get to know more about yourself and your motivations for investing.

Have a think about what drives you. Adventure, freedom, and experiences, like me? Goals, achievement, and excellence, like Cate? Or perhaps you're somewhere in between, driven by stability, security, and a low-risk outlook on life.

What's your purpose?

Once you've started to work out what drives you, the next question to ask yourself is, 'What do you want to achieve in life – what's your inner purpose?'

The great Stephen Covey wrote that a key habit of highly successful people is to begin with the end in mind. Taking action is great, but you need a strategy. The actions you take need to move you in the right direction, towards your ultimate destination. This requires a blueprint – a concept or vision of who and what you want to be – because things are created twice: once in the brain, and then a second time in physical reality.

It's startling how little consideration we tend to give to some of life's most fundamental issues, such as who we really are. Here are a few questions for you:

- What really lights you up? What are you genuinely passionate about?
- What do you do better than anyone else?
- What would you want people to say about you at your funeral?
- And importantly – *what do you do for people that changes their lives, and how does it change them?*

One way to identify your purpose – what's truly important to you – and think a bit more deeply about your life is to write a short personal mission statement. The finished article might be something as simple as this:

'My mission is to continually improve the quality of life of myself and my family, and to inspire others to follow me through helping and educating them.'

Most people will never trouble themselves to write a personal mission statement, and may even dismiss it as frightful bosh. But if you are one of the 70 per cent of people who find life unsatisfactory, perhaps you should.

Once you have an idea of your purpose in life, you know what you're investing in property for, what your boundaries and trade-offs can be, and that crucial piece of information: how much is enough. You'll also have a solid basis for making decisions about your career and business directions.

Freedom, money, and property

It goes without saying that there's much more to life than financial wealth. History is littered with wildly wealthy individuals who suffered personal tragedy, illness, sadness, or depression. Equally, many of the happiest, most purposeful, and most influential characters in history weren't rich in the traditional sense of the word.

We tend to associate the word 'wealth' with financial abundance, and this is one obvious measure of the term. There are three other types of wealth, however, that are less often considered:

1. **Social status**, or a sense of standing, is a form of wealth. We all like to have a role for ourselves in life, and having a sense of purpose is important, as we mentioned earlier – at the extreme

end of this spectrum, some will even become martyrs for their cause.

2. **Health** – each time we're ill or feel indisposed, we're reminded that all the money in the world is of limited use if we don't have our health, both physical and mental.
3. **Time freedom** is an increasingly precious commodity in the hectic modern world. As the great motivational speaker and author Jim Rohn once said, 'You can get more money, but you cannot get more time'.

You can see the potential trap here. An excessive focus on a career, business, or investment portfolio that might bring you the first two types of wealth – money and social status – might also rob you of your time and even your physical or mental wellbeing. As motivational speaker Denis Waitley said, 'Time and health are two precious assets we don't recognise and appreciate until they're depleted'.

What's the solution? We have limited control over our health, but we can make time to take the obvious preventative measures – eating well, exercising, getting check-ups, and looking after our mental wellbeing.

Is time freedom, then, actually the highest form of wealth? Is freedom the highest value? The ability to choose what you do, when you want to do it, and who you do it with is a precious privilege if you can achieve it.

About FIRE

In recent years we have seen the growth of the FIRE community – 'FIRE' stands for 'Financial Independence Retire Early'. FIRE sets freedom as the highest value of all – it encourages minimising spending, investing as much as possible as early as possible in income-producing assets such as shares, and then when the income exceeds your expenditure, you're free to go and do whatever takes your fancy.

It's a great concept, but it's up to the individual to decide whether they're happy to delay gratification and reduce spending on things like overseas travel.

Generally speaking, residential property is not the best asset class for generating income in the manner FIRE advocates. It takes a very long time to start seeing rents significantly exceeding your expenses, and even then, it's not the most efficient. There are three main advantages of property, however:

1. You can improve it, such as through renovations.
2. You can use more leverage to invest in a larger value portfolio sooner.
3. You can take a long-term approach to property investments with a view to capital growth. You can do this with share investments as well, of course, but in Australia, property has a history of providing great price growth.

Chapter 4 goes into much more detail on this.

How much is enough?

Your answer to the question, 'How much is enough?' is really about your purpose and your personal circumstances. A useful starting point is to work out how much money you want or need per annum, and then multiply this number by 25. This is called 'the 4 per cent rule', the idea being that you should be able to comfortably live off 4 per cent of your investment portfolio (that is, the portfolio divided by 25s) each year in retirement. Based on historical data, your money will most likely outlive you in this scenario!

There are plenty of different ways to reach this goal. One way for long-term 'buy and hold' property investors is to gradually pay down your mortgage debt over time, leaving you in the privileged position of living off the rental income without having to erode your equity by selling. Another strategy is to 'divest and reinvest', which is where you sell down your property assets and reinvest in a more liquid asset class such as shares. Some people might choose a hybrid model where they sell down some of their assets and retain some properties to generate rental income.

You can run the numbers yourself, or if you feel you need expert advice, you could consider paying a good financial advisor to help you. Don't forget to take into account superannuation and any likely government payments in your calculations. The Australian government has provided plenty of free resources to guide you on how much a comfortable retirement income might be at moneysmart.gov.au – this can be a useful starting point.

If you love your career or your business and don't necessarily want to retire early, property investing – Buying Right – is a terrific option. It can give you the freedom of choice and the ability to build wealth for future generations.

We talk more about the flip side of having 'enough' – when you never feel you have enough, no matter how much you achieve – in chapter 6.

Key points in this chapter

- Track down an Enneagram assessment and work out your personality type.
- Consider what your highest values and goals might be. Are you motivated by status, goals, and achievements? Are you motivated by freedom, experience, and adventure? Or, is financial stability your key objective?
- Understanding your personality type and goals is key to working out the ideal investment strategy for you.
- If you can find a career or business venture that you're passionate about, you'll likely to do it better and for longer.

3

What is the Buy Right Approach?

The Buy Right Approach is to carefully choose quality assets – buying right! – and then hold them as long as possible.

Buying property (or properties) is the single largest financial decision that most Aussies will ever make. Yet most people make up their property plans on the hoof! The Buy Right Approach is to be more conscientious: make a strategic plan, and then adjust course along the way as needed to deal with the inevitable challenges.

The future is somewhat unpredictable, but it still makes sense to build out a ten-year property plan to get the snowball rolling towards the 'enough' figure you calculated in chapter 2. Base the plan upon realistic assumptions, and remember to take into account your personality, values and purpose.

Your turn: creating your Buy Right plan

To create your Buy Right plan, work through these questions:

- *What is your retirement asset base and income stream goal?*
  For example, what retirement income do you wish to enjoy

directly from your property or wealth portfolio? Also, how many years of work do you have left before retirement? Some will adopt a buy-and-hold approach, while others will amass capital growth assets and sell some or all of them in retirement to reinvest in liquid assets to fund their retirement.

- *How many properties will you need to achieve your end goal?* Determining this will likely require the help of a mortgage broker, financial planner or property planner. The number of properties devised for a strategy is a function of the rental income or capital growth (equity) that the investor has defined as their retirement goal. For example, if we work off a gross rental yield of 3% for houses, and if an investor nominates a goal of $120,000 income from rent (in today's dollars) upon retirement, we can calculate that they will require a total portfolio value of $4 million. Pending servicing, timing and taxes, this could equate to four $1M properties, or five $800K properties, or eight $500,000 properties, and so on. Price and location diversification will need to be considered.

- *What financial metrics are you bound by, such as purchase price, required rental income, maximum outgoings or timeframe?* Some investors will have restrictions on borrowing at particular times of their lives – parental leave, new jobs, particular contracts, and so on – and some investors will be bound to a specific rental return, possibly at a higher level than 3% gross yield. This will determine some of the dwelling types and locations that the investor must target.

- *How long are you allowing for your assets to grow?* Investors start at different times in their lives, and the accumulation phase for a property portfolio can vary too. Some will amass assets in a tight timeframe, while others may spread out their timeframe. Obviously, those who start closer to their retirement phase allow less time for their assets to grow in capital value, but some will target higher yielding properties at this time in their life if retiring on rental income is their goal.

- *Are your goals achievable according to a finance professional?* Current incomes, future incomes, bonus payments and inheritances should all be considered when planning future acquisitions. Determining this will likely require the help of a mortgage broker, financial planner or property planner. Not every investor will be able to purchase at the frequency that they desire, and some will have to reduce their purchase-price goal if their current income doesn't service the debt.

- *What do you need to follow your plan?* Investors need to have a clear plan, mortgage strategy and realistic timeline in order to achieve their goals.

- *What performance can you reasonably expect?* Modelling asset growth at unrealistic levels leads to disappointment. Being aware of the historical growth of a particular dwelling type in a certain area, along with understanding the long-term rental yield of the asset, is important for modelling a reliable forecast.

- *How do you deal with setbacks and periods of limited credit availability?* Buffers, insurances and a long-term view are vital. Having the right advisors in place is critical to success.

- *What is your debt retirement strategy likely to be: buy and hold, or build, divest and reinvest in a more liquid asset class, such as shares?* Understanding the end goal is the most important piece of the puzzle. Without this, the strategy risks being undermined by the investor along the journey. For example, if buy and hold and strong rental yield is the endgame, there is little point comparing the assets in the portfolio to those of a high-capital-growth investor's portfolio; the two strategies are very different, and no two investors should expect identical outcomes.

You can use a simple spreadsheet if numbers are your thing, or there are handy online calculators and models that will give you a helping hand. We like GamePlans (www.gameplans.com.au) and the Australian Investment Property Calculator (investment propertycalculator.com.au).

What you should begin to notice is that if you achieve a constant rate of capital appreciation (price growth) over time, your equity or net worth will begin to curve nicely upwards over time. Our friend Stuart Wemyss of ProSolution Private Clients likes to demonstrate this in a nifty chart showing a property investment over 30 years (see figure 3.1). Note how the biggest chunk of the results come later in the investment period.

Figure 3.1: capital growth of a $500,000 property that increases in value by 8% p.a. over 30 years

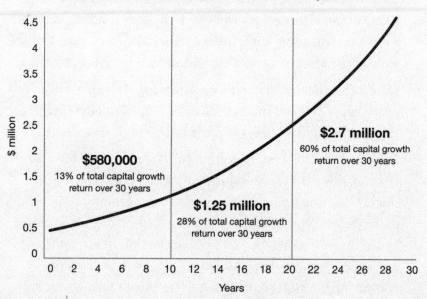

SOURCE: STUART WEMYSS, PROSOLUTION PRIVATE CLIENTS

The chart shows that, over time, you can achieve great things from a single, well-chosen property investment. Then, the hidden value in property as an investment asset class, as we've touched on earlier, is that after some price growth has been achieved, it's often possible to refinance some equity out of the property to use as a deposit to buy your next property.

If you can get two, three, four or more well-selected assets compounding away for you, then your wealth can begin to snowball magnificently. Of course, you must always manage the mortgage debt sensibly, and you need to be cognisant that interest rates will almost certainly move higher at various points along the journey.

Letting compound growth run wild

Legendary investor Charlie Munger, as mentioned before, once said that the first rule of compounding is never to interrupt it unnecessarily. He and investment partner Warren Buffett should know, having acquired the great bulk of their enormous wealth after the traditional retirement date!

Morgan Housel, in his brilliant book *The Psychology of Money*, also observes that the most impressive financial results tend to be achieved by people who allow compound interest to run wild for the longest period of time. The financial winners tend to be those who, on the one hand, don't succumb to greed and sell, and on the other hand, aren't spooked when their investment strategy has leaner years.

Warren Buffett is actually the perfect real-world example. In 1968, mathematician and investor Ed Thorp told his wife that Buffett would be the richest man in America one day, because of his intuitive understanding of how to compound his wealth. The interesting thing is that at the age of 52, Buffett's wealth was 'only' around US$376 million, yet at time of writing it is well over

US$100 billion. A great part of Buffett's secret is simply that he has been compounding his wealth for 80 years and counting!

All things being equal, the longer you hold a high-quality, high-performing investment, the more profit you'll make. The results in later years can be so strong as to be scarcely conceivable – in the words of nuclear physicist Albert Bartlett, 'The greatest shortcoming of the human race is our inability to understand the exponential function'. In financial terms, this roughly translates to:

> Find a strategy which can let compounding run wild for the longest possible period… and stick with it!

To pick out some examples of the long-term power of compound growth, you only have to look at property prices from 60 years ago and compare them to prices today. Prior to 1966, Australia was still using pounds instead of dollars, but you can still see the point being illustrated in the following newspaper clipping (see figure 3.2). Prices can be around 50 times higher today – and don't forget most real estate is bought using leverage (borrowed money), which magnifies the returns.

While there are some holding costs involved in property, the capital growth in Sydney and Melbourne over the 53 years after 1970 was in the region of 6000 per cent! Of course, the cost of living has increased too, but still these are powerful returns.

Are there any costs of strong long-term returns? Not really, but the 'price of entry' includes short-term fluctuations, volatility, endless media doom and gloom and sob stories about the ups and downs of markets. The sad thing is that this reporting of market cycles causes so much fear that many people become paralysed and never take any action. Over the long term it costs them so much. We talk about this more in chapter 5.

Figure 3.2: houses for sale in January 1965

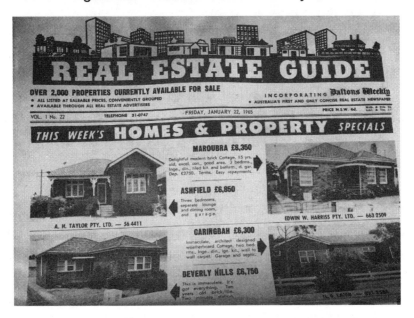

However, think back to what you were doing ten years ago and how much life has changed for you since that time. You may begin to get a sense of how tough it is to design an investment strategy that you can stick to for the long term. Herein lies the challenge, and something for us to contemplate together as we work through this book:

> How can you allow the power of compound growth to flourish for the longest possible period?

Start compounding today – it is, quite literally, about time.

Fads vs survivors

The Dutch-born commodities trader Ed Seykota once quipped, 'There are old traders and there are bold traders, but there are no old, bold traders'. You may be able to take wild risks at times, especially at a young age, but it's not a sustainable way to build wealth over the long term.

In recent years, we've seen a spate of new traders and speculators roaring into financial and property markets with extremely high levels of confidence, while some of the more experienced investors have become a little more circumspect. Most likely, these young investors are being emboldened by the short-term rises in their portfolios, while older investors have seen this movie before and are therefore adopting a more prudent approach. While the initial quote was more related to stock markets, there is one constant in investment markets, and that is human nature. If you're going to invest for the long term – for decades – then you want to stick to tried-and-tested strategies that have delivered consistent results for decades in the past and will continue to do so for decades into the future.

An analogy here: American bombers returning from European raids during World War II were found to be peppered with bullet holes, providing invaluable data for the analysts. They realised that they needed to focus on reinforcing the areas of the planes that had no bullet holes – the engines! The planes that had survived and returned to base had taken no hits to their engines, and this was what had kept them flying.

Success leaves clues, as they say, so we should look at the attributes of outstanding investments, investors, mentors, and businesses that have been around for a long time – those with a proven track record. But we shouldn't forget to consider what's no longer around! Poor businesses with fatal weaknesses don't tend to stick around for too long, so it can be easy to overlook what hasn't worked.

In the same way, expert property commentators will never be shy about highlighting their best predictions, but human nature dictates they won't be so forthcoming about their more underwhelming calls. So, apply a healthy scepticism. Investment fads come and go all the time. In property investing, for example, mining towns were all the rage for a few years before demand crashed. Then there has been flipping, granny flats, dual tenancies, and plenty more besides!

Don't get sidetracked: stick with what's proven, and do what works! Invest in the best-quality properties you can afford and hold them for as long as possible. Desirable property elements may include, for example, a high level of amenity while not being in a noisy locale, a well-regarded street, a desirable orientation, a well-proportioned and designed floor plan, and a well-maintained property.

On buying new properties and the Lindy effect

Statistically, it's riskier to invest in new properties, such as house and land packages or off-the-plan apartments. Cate and I know this through industry experience, but the facts are in the public domain. Every year the figures are published, showing that a significant number of people lose money buying brand-new properties. In the extreme cases, some new apartments in this latest (at the time of writing) construction cycle in Sydney have even been deemed structurally unsafe and are now worthless.

There's an old rule of thumb in the world of economics that the longer something has been around, the longer it's likely to stick around.

I'm not a boozer these days, but in my early twenties there was never any need to ask me what drink I wanted for the next round – it was always a pint of Guinness, no questions asked! Lots of trendy new ales came and went, as did various fads such as alcopops and the like, but nothing compared to the smooth black drop with a frothy shamrock atop. Guinness has been brewed since 1759, and I wouldn't mind a bet that it'll still be enjoyed by glowing customers for centuries to come.

In a similar vein, my kids love Disney movies, just as other children before them have for decades. And doubtless when high school comes around, they'll be studying Shakespeare just as I did, and my old man before me, and his dad before him.

The longer things have been around, the longer you expect them to be around. This is known as the Lindy effect. Perishable goods and people have a life expectancy, of course – sadly, we tend to deteriorate with age! But for some non-perishables – such as brands or technologies – each additional period of survival implies a mortality rate that is decreasing over time. Figure 3.3 illustrates the point.

Figure 3.3: the Lindy effect

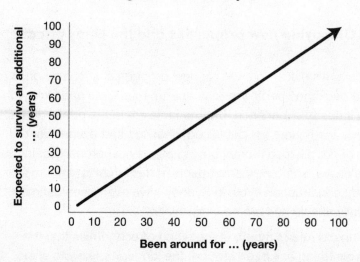

How is this relevant to investing? Because you can narrow down your choice of investments to the most durable assets classes and businesses. This method was explored more deeply by Nassim Taleb in his terrific book *Antifragile: Things that gain from disorder.*

The Lindy effect helps to explain why experienced investors such as Warren Buffett place a far greater emphasis on the earnings of well-established businesses than the results of ventures that have only been around for a few short years.

In real estate, we've taken great comfort in investing in inner-Sydney's Victorian terraces or well-established boutique unit blocks. You need to be wary of issues such as damp and termites, but we've frequently taken the view that what's been scarce and popular for a century will probably still be scarce and popular a century from now.

On the other hand, I look at some of the towers sprouting up around Sydney airport or out near the Olympic stadium, and it's tough to gauge with any certainty how they'll fare over the next few years, let alone the next 100 years!

If you *must* buy new property, as some non-resident buyers must for legal reasons, you can at least look to apply the Lindy effect principle to the development company: look for reputable developers that have been around through several property cycles, as they'll probably be around for several more.

Key points in this chapter

- The most powerful force in the investing universe is compound growth.
- Work towards a strategy of letting compound growth work for you uninterrupted for the longest possible period.
- Don't get sidetracked by fads. Stick to what's been proven to work!
- Buying new property is statistically riskier than buying established property.

4

Why property?

You've heard our stories now, you've done some thinking about who you are and what you want, and you've learned about the basics of the Buy Right Approach, but you might still have one question:

Why property? Why not shares or other assets?

Because property creates more millionaires than any other asset class. There are four main reasons, which we touched on earlier:

1. You can be above-average at property investing.
2. You can use leverage.
3. Property has had solid long-term returns.
4. Property can be improved with effort (such as through renovation or rezoning).

Let's look at each of these in a bit more detail.

You can be above-average

You can do better than average in property because most people in the market don't even try to! Most people only buy property to live in, and even most 'investors' buy without much thought, then often become disillusioned and sell.

As we've mentioned before, it's amazing how little time and attention people generally put into a property purchase, given that for most people it's the single biggest financial investment they ever make! Punters frequently buy blindly or based on emotion, giving very little thought to strategy or the potential negative outcomes if they get it wrong. Almost anyone can finish in an exceptionally strong position, however, just by following a few simple rules and making a few smart decisions.

The other reason it's not hard to be above-average at property investing is that there are always opportunities to negotiate bargains, buy in a gentrifying hotspot, or add value through renovations or development (which we explore in more detail later in this chapter). By contrast, it can be hard to find a bargain-priced share (and impossible to personally add value unless you work at that company), since publicly available information about a company is quickly reflected in its share price.

Long-term leverage

The second reason we choose property is leverage – being able to borrow the bank's money to invest larger sums, and pay them off over a long period like a 25- or 30-year mortgage term.

It is possible to invest for the long term in the stock market, but most people buy and sell far too often, and it's much harder for the average investor to use the same level of leverage safely. Loans to buy shares, called 'margin loans', come with much higher risk due to how much the price of shares can change day to day. If the loan-to-value ratio on your margin loan falls below your lender's specified percentage, they will call on you to add more funds to the loan to get the percentage back under their target. This is called a 'margin call' and can be a very unpleasant surprise.

With property, the ability to invest for the long term allows compound growth to deliver increasingly higher returns over time. This combination of leverage and compounding growth is what makes property so powerful. This is the exciting part, when you combine these two wonders of finance to accelerate your results.

The 'rule of 72' tells you how long an asset takes to double in value given a consistent annual growth rate. For example, if an asset were to increase in value by 7 per cent per annum, it would take about a decade to double in value (72 ÷ 7 = 10.3 years). Intuitively, you might expect an asset which increases in value at a rate of 10 per cent per annum would take a decade to double in value. But because the dollar value increases get larger every year, it only takes 7.2 years (72 ÷ 10 = 7.2 years).

If you use, say, a $50,000 deposit to invest in a $500,000 property, and it doubles in value, who gets to own the increased value of the property? You do! There may be other costs to take into account, such as stamp duty, legal fees, and some running costs, but the principle is the important thing here, which is that the $50,000 deposit has created more than $500,000 of equity over time, or more than ten times the initial investment.

A word of caution: don't borrow more than you can comfortably afford to repay. Banks are more cautious about lending than they once were, but you could still get yourself in trouble if you're not careful.

It's also important to note that leverage works both ways, and if the property you invest in declines in value, then the losses are also magnified. This is why we're determined to drill home the Buy Right Approach to investing and to get investors focused on the long term. As we said at the start of the book, property tends to be a very forgiving asset class over the long run – as long as you buy well.

Solid long-term returns

Great long-term returns are the third reason we love property investing. Property has had long-term capital growth returns of 8 to 10 per cent per annum through booms and recessions, wars, border closures, good times, bad times, global depressions, pandemics, periods of high inflation and interest rates, periods of low inflation and interest rates, and everything else.

Just as importantly, property prices in Australian capital cities (and in some regional cities within a couple of hours of a major capital city) have outperformed inflation over time – meaning that the net value of the property has increased beyond that of inflation. Inflation is the change in price of a collection of 'typical' goods and services purchased by a household: it's a measure of how much prices are rising. In other words, even accounting for general price rises, the property is more valuable than when it was purchased.

It's true that some people have lost money in property, but it's usually for one of three main reasons: they buy poorly, they sell too soon, or they overcommit to a loan that they're ultimately unable to meet the repayments on and are forced to sell in a market downturn.

However, almost everyone who has invested soundly for the long term in Australian property has seen handsome returns and built wealth. There used to be a trope in property seminars decades ago that property prices have doubled every decade since 1086 and the Domesday Book. Is that a myth? We're not sure, as the records are very sketchy once you go back more than a century or so. However, we have reasonable data from more recent times – take a look at figure 4.1, for example, showing how house prices fared in Australia from 1970 to 2021.

Is it possible that property prices may not rise as steeply in the future as they have in the past? In short, yes, and we get into that in chapter 11. However, the important thing is to invest in quality assets which have the best possible chance of outperforming inflation and making you money over the long term.

Figure 4.1: house prices in Australia from 1970 to 2021

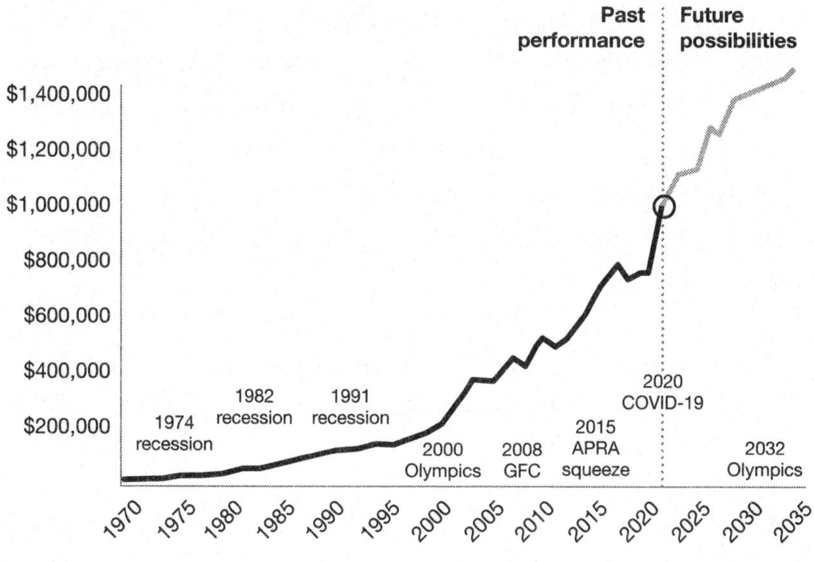

SOURCE: PROPERTYOLOGY

Why do property prices go up?

Why do property prices rise? Well, for a number of reasons:

- Rising incomes drive land prices higher in popular suburbs over the years.

- Construction costs also tend to rise over time, as the price of materials and construction wages increases relentlessly. The costs of building a new dwelling have actually soared far and away above inflation over the past six decades, due to dramatic increases in the size and quality of homes; the volume of regulation; and the costs of site clearance, remediation, and preparation. It has become generally more expensive to produce new housing, even on greenfield sites (new housing estates on former farmland) which are flat and easy to build on.

· Australia is also a high-population-growth country, and over time this growth pushes up the price of land, especially in the landlocked suburbs of the cities where most Aussies and new arrivals want to live. Take a look at the long-range projections for some of the main capital cities in Australia shown in figure 4.2. Over the long term, the population is forecast to continue to grow, and grow, and grow. It adds up to massive demand for housing.

Figure 4.2: long-range population projections of selected Australian cities, 1901 to 2061

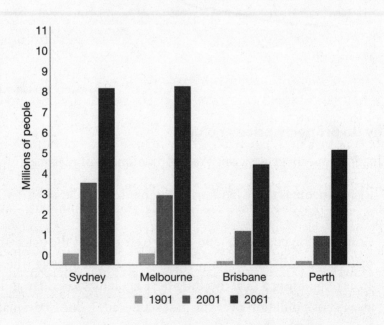

SOURCE: AUSTRALIAN BUREAU OF STATISTICS; BERNARD SALT, *THE AUSTRALIAN*

Living standards, stocks and jolly hockey sticks

We often see charts that show apparently never-ending 'hockey stick' style growth, including when it comes to living standards. A longer-term look at growth in the global economy per person ('GDP per capita') plotted on a logarithmic scale would show that there were long, drawn-out stretches through history where living standards barely improved at all. But from around the time of the industrial revolution things really took off (and then some!).

Looking at real GDP per capita, you could certainly make the case that the rate of growth may be slowing a bit since the early 1980s, especially after the coronavirus recession of 2020. Growth rates notwithstanding, most optimists would say that thanks to overall technological advancement, living standards will continue to rise at a consistent pace for decades into the future.

How does this translate to businesses (and therefore to stocks)? It's quite common for younger businesses to present charts showing or projecting 'hockey stick' growth in their customer bases and revenues, but relatively few established businesses can sustain genuine compound growth for long periods of time.

The online retailer Amazon is a rare and outstanding example of a business that has continued to experience compound growth in its revenue and customer base; it has expanded into new markets with new products, partly by eschewing the drive for bottom-line profits. Many companies can increase their revenue over time, but very few are able to continue compounding at a constant rate for a long period, let alone at Amazon's mind-bending rate. And, judging solely from the volume of parcels arriving at our places lately, Amazon is going to keep growing for some years to come!

However, as mentioned, the reality is that Amazon is the exception to the rule: for most businesses, ultimately a growth plateau beckons.

OK, great... so what about property?

Buy land: they're not making it anymore

Folks generally like the security of real estate because returns tend to be less volatile, and there's a sense of it being a perpetual investment – like humans, companies have a life cycle, but land can't easily be moved or destroyed.

Two of the oldest adages of real estate are 'Location, location, location' and 'Find out where people are moving to, and buy the land before they get there'. In our experience, these have a lot of truth in them. Land may be the greatest investment of all, but it's got to be in the right location, otherwise the results may be underwhelming.

Economist and academic Robert Shiller showed that in the USA, residential real estate prices over the very long term had appreciated only by a modest percentage per annum above the rate of inflation. This intuitively makes sense, although the leveraged returns from some markets (such as Manhattan) would've been better than others (such as Detroit).

As someone who was born in Sheffield, a resources city where the regional population declined as the steel industry and coal mines closed, Pete is aware of the risks of investing in cites which are heavily reliant upon one industry. Australia has had its own examples over recent decades through the resources investment boom and bust years.

The US city of Detroit has been one of the most extreme examples of this in recent decades. The population of Detroit exploded to 1.85 million in the 1950s as the car-manufacturing industry boomed, making it the fifth largest city in the USA. However, as the car industry declined, Detroit suffered severe urban decay. The population declined by two-thirds from the late 20th century to sit at around 630,000 today, resulting in vacant blocks and dilapidated housing everywhere. The average home price in Detroit declined from nearly $98,000 in 2003 to just $13,638 in 2009.

We are fortunate in Australia that, as a high-population-growth country, we haven't experienced anything as extreme as this in recent decades. In Britain, though, we've seen first-hand the risks of investing in towns and cities with struggling industries. The most reliable long-term growth and returns tend to come from larger cities with strong growth across a well-diversified range of industries.

In Australia, most of the population lives within two hours of Greater Sydney, Melbourne, or Brisbane. These areas continue to grow in popularity, with employment opportunities available across many industries. Here's the key point:

Australia is a vast country. Land, overall, isn't a scarce commodity – but in some landlocked neighbourhoods it is.

Compound growth in real estate is most likely to come from areas where there is:

- a scarcity of well-located land
- a growing population and a growing demand
- inherited wealth which tends to be capitalised into land values.

It seems to us that in outer-suburban or distant regional real-estate markets, where land is less scarce and where marginal prices are set by younger or first-time buyers, genuine compound growth over the long term is unlikely to occur. This is especially true these days, as technology and modular construction make tract or 'cookie-cutter' housing more efficient to produce.

Gentrification

One of the most profitable property investment strategies is to buy in cheaper locations that you believe are set to gentrify and become more popular. This requires some research and a bit of vision – it can be hard to visualise an ugly-duckling suburb becoming a beautiful swan in the future, though there are plenty of examples.

Everyone loves to back a winner, particularly when it comes to investing in property. And everyone would love to identify a suburb that is set to take off, get in ahead of the crowd and enjoy strong capital growth. So, what is gentrification, and how does it affect property prices in a suburb?

Gentrification is normally understood to be a new class of people moving into a location, leading to the area becoming more popular or 'trendy'. A suburb which was once looked down upon or out of favour thus becomes more sought-after.

Gentrifying suburbs are often lower socio-demographic suburbs, areas that initially had plenty of light industry, or locations where working-class or blue-collar jobs dominated. These suburbs transform over time as bargain-hunting creatives and then aspirational young professionals move in.

The legendary 'Property Professor' Peter Koulizos conducted extensive research into what makes a suburb likely to gentrify. He found that likely suburbs tend to have a number of historic buildings (not simply a proliferation of industrial sheds!) and are usually located close to either the city or the water.

Think of the already gentrified suburbs you know, and you will find that his research is borne out. In Sydney, for example, Erskineville, Newtown, Enmore, Marrickville, Alexandria, Paddington, and Redfern are all close to the city. There are hipsters seemingly everywhere you look in such suburbs these days!

 Balmain tap-dancing

When I first came to Sydney back in the 1990s, my cricketing mates still used the phrase 'Balmain tap-dancing' – which as far as I understood it was slang for people getting a good shoeing in a rough pub (though I willingly stand to be corrected!). In any case, the residents of Balmain these days are far more likely to engage in actual tap-dancing. The suburb has long since gentrified enormously, with a beautiful main strip offering craft beers, cakes, and character on practically every corner.

In Melbourne, Richmond and St Kilda have gentrified significantly over the years. Similarly in Brisbane, suburbs such as West End and New Farm would fit the bill as gentrified suburbs, being close to the water and the city.

I lived in New Farm in Brisbane for a good few years myself: it's famous for having a café on every corner, with easy ferry or cycleway access to the city. With the $5 million homes and multi-million-dollar apartments these days, it can be hard to imagine that New Farm was once a rough and rundown locale, before Italian migrants moved in and upgraded the suburb in characteristic style.

What are the signs that a suburb is undergoing gentrification? Much of what we perceive to be gentrification is visual: more homes being renovated; smarter cars in the driveways; less litter; new murals; cafés, trendy bars and restaurants popping up; former warehouses being converted into swanky new apartments.

As the demographics change, the locals will increasingly be seen exercising in the parks and green spaces, jogging enthusiastically in the streets, cycling to coffee shops in the all the latest gear and choosing between soy, oat, almond and regular milk for their lattes! A new gym or two may open in the suburb, alongside vegetarian eateries or health food stores.

What are some of the data indicators to look out for? One of the key pieces of data *is a rise in dual-income households*, as aspirational young professionals move in. There may also be an increase in artists or creatives, who traditionally tend to flock towards the more affordable inner-city areas, kick-starting the change in demographics from blue collar to middle class. The demographics will shift over time to reflect the new arrivals to the suburb, often young graduates, professionals, entrepreneurs, or white-collar employees. The best place to research demographic information such as this is the Australian Bureau of Statistics website, which is a treasure trove of information, including the Australian Census data.

For property owners and buyers, gentrification means, most obviously, increasing popularity and competition pushing up land and property values, as professionals compete for well-located but affordable real estate.

Gentrifying suburbs can be a great option for first homebuyers, who can buy in a relatively cheap suburb with the likelihood of being able to trade up as their incomes and home values increase. Investors can potentially enjoy capital growth, rising rents, and the option to renovate and add further value later, perhaps creating a finished-article home to be sold on to a family buyer later in the property cycle.

Are there any downsides to investing in a gentrifying suburb? There can be some genuine social issues relating to gentrification, such as the displacement of existing residents, or unwanted changes to the community's culture and character. The transition may not always be smooth, as we have sometimes seen in Sydney when public housing has been sold off to the detriment of the incumbent tenants. And if you invest early in the gentrification process, it may be tricky to land a secure tenancy while the demand for rentals is still low.

Similarly, when an area is undergoing significant development, with older homes being pulled down to make way for medium-density townhouses and apartments, then there could be an oversupply of new properties in the suburb... at least temporarily.

However, when well-informed investors have bought houses strategically in gentrifying suburbs, they've often seen a doubling (and sometimes more) of property values over the course of a decade.

This is how to get in early

How, then, can you identify gentrifying suburbs before they become too expensive to invest in?

First, start by looking up the most affordable suburbs close to the city or close to the water in the city in which you are interested. Median house price data by suburb can be your guide here, for an initial screening of potential candidate suburbs.

Second, look at the census and other suburb data for employment and income trends, and look at changes in demographics. Are incomes increasing? Are there more professionals? Are there more two-income households?

Third, get out from behind the desk and take a look for yourself. We may be biased, but we reckon there is no substitute for getting out there and treading the streets. The soft indicators of a genuinely gentrifying suburb will suddenly become more than evident to you, especially if you can chat to a few locals about what is happening in the area... the good and the bad!

If you're planning to invest in a gentrifying suburb, should you buy a rundown property in need of renovation, or should you buy a fully renovated property?

There's no right or wrong answer here, but your timing will be key. At the time of writing, materials costs are very high and tradies are often in short supply, after the previous government's 'HomeBuilder' stimulus and the associated construction boom. The best bang for your buck may therefore be to invest in a property which is in good enough condition to rent out to a young family or young professionals today, but with future potential to add value or renovate in the future. This approach is neatly encapsulated by the phrase 'equity on ice'.

Property can be improved

Property can be financially improved with effort. We've just discussed renovation, but improvements can also be made through new builds or developments, or town planning changes. The latter may not necessarily be created by the owner – in fact, many advantageous town planning changes are a result of urban growth and are a case of good luck for property owners. Take, for example, a rezoning that enhances the development opportunity of a particular area: this can add significant value to a property in a very short period of time.

*

As you can see, there are excellent reasons to choose property as an investment, and to maintain an attitude of cautious optimism. Let's look at that further, in chapter 5.

Key points in this chapter

- It's not hard to be above-average at property investing.
- Property prices have compounded at around 8 to 10 per cent per annum over many decades. Future capital growth may well be lower, but so too will be the increase in the cost of living and interest rates.
- There's a scarcity of sought-after blocks of land in many landlocked suburbs and neighbourhoods.
- Look for tried-and-tested locations with a long track record of delivering consistently compounding capital growth.
- A good way to start might be to look for affordable suburbs set to gentrify.

5

Be cautiously optimistic

Optimists tend to fare better than pessimists in property investment, largely because prices mostly go up over the long term. Of course, you do need to be careful with the use of debt, and ideally you should aim to take advantage of market cycles by investing when prices are attractive.

The problem with being too pessimistic is that you're always looking for the next thing to go wrong, which can lead to panicked reactions and, often, selling too soon. The average hold period for an investment property has now increased to close to ten years, but many investors still sell much sooner.

One of the greatest advantages (and disadvantages) of real estate as an investment is that it's relatively illiquid. While stock market investors can buy and sell at the click of a button, it's much harder to do in property. Pete, for example, has never sold a property. Despite often thinking about it after a market boom cycle, the idea of paying transaction costs and capital gains tax always puts him off. When he prepares his tax return, it's amazing to see all these assets that were bought 5, 10, 15 or even 25 years ago.

The average holding period for stock market investments, by contrast, is measured in months these days, at well under a year. People are constantly buying and selling in a vain attempt to beat the market, which most people never do. Ironically enough, this is at least partially due to the costs of buying and selling.

Gloomy forecasts, always and everywhere

In May 2020, when the coronavirus hit Australia, the doom and gloom forecasts came thick and fast. And how! One headline read as follows:

> 'House prices could fall 32 per cent under "prolonged" slump: CBA'

Rewind to 2019, and this time around it was the Aussie election causing ructions. This quote is from *The Guardian:*

> 'The downturn has prompted Torsten Slok, Deutsche Bank's chief international economist, to list the Australian housing market as one of the top 30 economic risks to look out for in 2019.
>
> 'A "house price crash in Australia and Canada" ranks alongside a no-deal Brexit, the US government shutdown, and the escalation of the US-China trade war.'

Before that, in 2017 and 2018, there was concern that the Royal Commission into banking misconduct could freeze up credit and lead to a wave of forced sales. ABC News reported that 'Australia is in a property downturn that rivals 1989'.

Of course, in the era of online media, where clicks are currency, you can predict practically anything in any year, and there are always gloomy predictions of recessions and a housing market crunch.

In 2011, the *Sydney Morning Herald* warned of a 'Record slump in house prices in 2011':

'Australian house prices plunged by the most on record in 2011 as global economic uncertainty and concerns about its impact at home kept a lid on demand.'

A trawl through the archives shows that the pre-internet era wasn't much different. For example, in 2003, the media and IMF warned about a dangerous property bubble following Sydney's 2000 Olympics boom. Reading these articles from decades ago – with their warnings about affordability, first homebuyers being locked out, and the inevitable downturns to follow – you often get the sense that they could have been written yesterday.

We could go on and on… but you get the picture. If you believe the media, it's basically never a good time to invest in property.

Optimism wins

Household wealth has continued to explode in Australia over recent decades to around $15 trillion in 2023, up from around $1 billion four decades ago. The population has increased significantly over time, but remarkably, Credit Suisse reports that the median adult wealth per capita in Australia is the highest in the world.

Partly, that's because Aussies invest plenty for their retirement via compulsory superannuation. It's also because stocks have performed well, as Aussies benefited hugely from their growing pension balances. And of course, a large part of the wealth of Australian households has been created by the housing market. The total value of the residential housing market is around $10 trillion at the time of writing, up from $5 trillion in 2014.

It's well known that stock markets and housing markets move in cycles. Importantly, however, most investors aren't very good at timing those market cycles accurately. For that reason, optimists have generally fared far better than pessimists, who are always waiting for the sky to fall.

We have both mentored and bought properties for clients who have made themselves multi-millionaires simply by making a few smart decisions and holding investments for the long term. We've even come across 'accidental millionaires' who've created huge wealth in their family homes and superannuation investments.

The flip side to this is that we know of pessimists who are constantly waiting for the world to end. Every time the economy suffers a slowdown, or a market takes a downturn, they're always the first to say, 'I told you so'; yet somehow they never seem to pull the trigger on a successful investment, despite always believing themselves to be smarter than the crowd.

We're not talking here about being gung-ho or taking stupid risks. Rather, we are recognising that to create wealth in a remarkably successful country such as Australia, we need to be aware of the long-term market trends and work within those parameters.

Sometimes good or bad luck can play a part, and often life gets in the way. Statistically, for example, most Aussies will have more than one de facto relationship these days, and sometimes a separation can result in what's euphemistically known as an 'asset reallocation program'. Similarly, people can lose their jobs during a recession, which may result in financial difficulties.

At business and wealth seminars, we've seen exercises where people are asked to draw a graph or chart of the ups and downs through their adult life. It's amazing how often we seem to have at least one major 'down' period in our lives, and sometimes several. That's to be expected. The important thing is not to become a pessimist, but to cling on to optimism and resolve to bounce back.

In business, the economy, and life, winter is followed by summer. We can't control luck, but we can position ourselves sensibly and strategically, and we can control the way we respond to what happens to us.

 ## Outrageous good fortune during the pandemic

Let's circle back to a recent period of outrageous good fortune for some property owners: the pandemic and its impact on some regional areas in Australia. Who was to know that a virus would have such a catastrophic impact on the world? From horrendous death tolls to overstretched healthcare facilities, mental health impacts, and business closures, COVID-19 certainly left a trail of devastation in its wake.

Unexpectedly, though, there were positive impacts for some – online retailers for example – and indeed, for some Australian property owners, as you can see from figure 5.1. And take this eye-popping statistic from CoreLogic:

> 'National dwelling values rose 28.6% from September 2020 to April 2022'

Figure 5.1: total value of dwelling stock in Australia

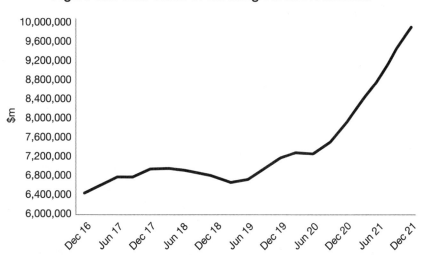

SOURCE: AUSTRALIAN BUREAU OF STATISTICS, RESIDENTIAL PROPERTY PRICE INDEXES: EIGHT CAPITAL CITIES DECEMBER 2021

The difference between capital-city performance and regional-city performance was dramatic, however, even amid a host of well-performing markets.

In our southern states – particularly South Australian regional locations – plenty of investors generated some serious equity in a short space of time. Notably, many of these investors would have been enjoying low holding costs (and likely low mortgages) during this stellar period of growth.

I met many accidental investors who suddenly found themselves with serious gains during 2022 and 2023 after these lockdown boltholes bolstered the value of their overall portfolios. One particular investor that comes to mind is a first homebuyer who purchased a seemingly lacklustre off-the-plan apartment in Victoria's Surf Coast town of Torquay. According to an industry friend who was privy to the purchase, this first homebuyer beat the odds and not only settled a purchase with positive equity, but had a bank valuation that pointed to a gain in value of over 60 per cent for the new apartment within just three years of signing a contract to purchase. *60 per cent!*

Could that result ever be replicated? Perhaps not, but this first homebuyer could have crystallised the gain and been able to springboard into something closer to a metro city if she'd been so inclined.

Which leads me to another story closer to home. I had two older clients who had dreamed of life in a luxury St Kilda Road apartment. For those of you familiar with Melbourne's inner-ring market, you can imagine the view from such an apartment: superb vistas across Albert Park lake or overlooking some of the botanic gardens, with trams running by and fairy lights glistening at night.

The couple in question owned a modest little house in Mornington Peninsula's Tootgarook. During the lockdown period, a glut of Melburnian escapees flooded the peninsula in search of space, safety, security, and a life that they felt they could enjoy, outside the then-depressing city.

Melbourne city was a ghost town. Friends who live in the inner-city referred to it as 'the zombie apocalypse'. Nobody wanted to reside in town, high-rise living became nigh on impossible due to restrictions on lift usage, most of the international students had returned home, and every shop was closed. It was very eerie.

Interest rates were at an all-time low, and many people purchased holiday homes or made a permanent sea-change at this time. Values soared and local agents struggled to keep up with the volume of buyers. In smaller markets, relatively small changes in the number of buyers can result in remarkable changes in prices. Most were buying sight unseen via an online auction process that could only be described as irrational.

In late 2021, our clients traded out of their house in Tootgarook, managing the sales campaign online with livestream video and sight-unseen buyers. In tandem, I negotiated hard on a superbly appointed three-bedroom apartment with gorgeous city views. In hindsight, they timed it perfectly. Their apartment purchase price was negatively impacted by COVID-19 lockdowns, while the price they got for their coastal home was higher than could be achieved now.

Stories like this strike me as examples of stunning good fortune!

As we mentioned earlier, of course not all purchases go swimmingly, and being mindful of unforeseen surprises and issues is important; illness, natural disasters and job losses are among just a few that can cause mortgage stress. Having suitable insurances in place is essential. We cover 'managing debt' in chapter 6.

 ## Ignoring interest-rate white noise

My second property purchase was in 2000, and I still recall the comments that people in my circle of influence made. Interest rates were climbing, and for those who had experienced the challenges of the 1990s when interest rates exceeded 17 per cent, I must have seemed cavalier. The purchase price and estimated returns were manageable, though, and I shook off the white noise and ploughed ahead with the purchase. The house was particularly rugged, but the land was fabulous – 646 square metres just a few minutes from the beach in the Melbourne bayside suburb of Seaford – and all my reading had taught me that it's well-located land that appreciates over time.

My then-husband and I tidied the house up and lived in it as our principal place of residence; then, just two years later, we sold it for close to double the purchase price! One could argue that I timed it well, and certainly, at the time I felt so clever turning such an amazing profit. In hindsight, though, that sale was one of my silliest rookie mistakes. Take a look at its sales history:

- **20 May 1977:** Sold for $27,000
- **1 November 1987:** Sold for $58,000
- **9 August 2000:** Sold for $97,000
- **2 September 2002:** Sold for $180,000
- **24 November 2006:** Sold for $450,000
- **16 November 2020:** Sold for $1,060,000.

Yep. The property was a fantastic long-term keeper, yet I liquidated it. It was a painful lesson! The land was subsequently redeveloped, but even taking into account the cost of a basic home build, the gains would have been substantial.

That acquisition and divestment got me thinking, though, and I learned a valuable lesson from that mistaken sale as I tracked subsequent sales over the years in this pocket of Seaford, I realised that most of the real benefits of investing come from *time in the market,* rather than *timing the market*. Had I held onto this asset (which had a debt of just $20,000 on it by the time it was sold), it would have been worth more than $1 million today.

The other lesson from this purchase was that ignoring interest rate chatter and thinking long term – as opposed to trying to fine-tune or time cycles and interest rate movements – pays off.

I've plotted the Seaford purchase and two other examples from my investing experience on figure 5.2, which shows Australia's cash rate (the interest rate set each month by the Reserve Bank of Australia). I then looked retrospectively at their respective performance since the date of acquisition.

Figure 5.2: Australia's cash rate from 1990 to 2020

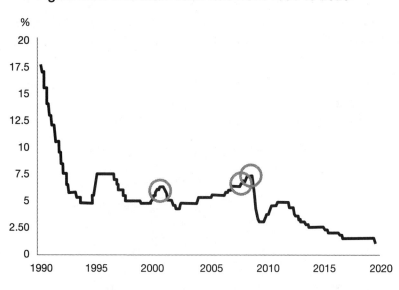

SOURCE: RBA

The first circle from the left of the chart, around the year 2000, indicates my short period of ownership of the Seaford property.

The next circle marks the first self-managed superannuation fund (SMSF) purchase my husband and I made together. I was working in finance at the time and excitedly took advantage of the opportunity to borrow within the fund to purchase real property. It should come as little surprise, of course, to hear that I was warned against such an idea by others! Red-brick, four-bedroom Hobart beauty *Welona* was purchased in June 2008 for $560,000 (see figure 5.3, overleaf). This was the closest to a capital-city-centre period home that I could identify at the time within my budget. (I discuss this purchase further in chapter 6.)

Welona's proximity to the city centre has paid dividends – the house has never had a single day of vacancy. The rental at the time I write this is $760 per week, and the estimated capital growth has been 6 per cent per annum. Hobart has delivered exceptional capital growth of late, although it's fair to say that we also sat through a very static period for some years. The long-term hold strategy has ultimately rewarded this investment decision, which hinged on a combination of growth and yield – although, having said that, interest-rate cycles haven't significantly influenced its performance. Retiring the SMSF debt (that is, paying it off) was our secondary intention for this house.

Figure 5.3: *Welona*, the Hobart-based SMSF acquisition

The last circle on the chart is interesting. The little weatherboard, semi-detached beachside cottage in Aspendale, Melbourne – shown in figure 5.4 – was purchased in December 2008 for

$310,000, as global financial crisis fears were rattling through the nation and the Reserve Bank of Australia was bracing for an emergency interest-rate cut. I remember every outspoken piece of advice we were given about the impending market collapse, and in particular, being told that the timing was terrible for this purchase.

Figure 5.4: the Aspendale beach house

Interest rates had been climbing, and looking at the chart, we bought this property at the highest cash-rate peak of the current century! Regardless, this little property has delivered an annualised capital growth return of over 8 per cent per annum and was cashflow neutral (meaning the income and costs cancelled each other out) within the first few years of ownership. The impact of a long-term hold strategy, and of disregarding media white noise, cannot be overestimated.

It's essential, of course, to ensure you consider affordability and have cashflow and healthy buffers in place. Once that's done, though, focusing on hype and headlines just steals time from investors who want to start their investment journey.

Be approximately right, not precisely wrong

One of the big accounting firms got our goat recently when it released house price growth forecasts. The forecasts, by capital city, predicted growth for years into the future to the 'accuracy' of one decimal point. Even if you could predict the future of housing markets to a decimal point – which you can't – what does a percentage change at the city level even mean for individual property owners? In short, not much!

This type of forecast is released all the time. The media runs with them verbatim because they're precise and can produce a compelling narrative... and even if they're proven to be completely wrong, people will have forgotten by then!

It's simple enough to build 'as if' models, and they can be alluring because they give precise predictions. There's just one problem: the real world gets in the way, and the assumptions often don't hold up in real-life situations! The future is inherently uncertain, so all models and forecasts need to be questioned. In some respects, the more you know, the more you don't know.

Rather than precise projections, the most important thing is a high level of accuracy in asking and then answering the right questions. High accuracy, low precision, as illustrated in figure 5.5. It's clear that getting hung up on precise metrics and values can be self-defeating and isn't time well spent... so what is? Asking the wrong questions can be as bad as doing no research at all, so here are three questions that you should ask:

- Will people actually do what they say they will? All too often, they don't.
- What do your instincts tell you? Gut feel, while no replacement for hard information, can be a useful sense-checking tool.
- If the models and forecasts are wrong, what might happen instead?

Figure 5.5: accuracy versus precision

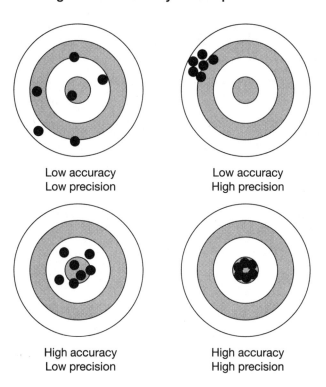

Low accuracy
Low precision

Low accuracy
High precision

High accuracy
Low precision

High accuracy
High precision

Don't sacrifice accuracy for illusory precision, and be prepared to update your views as new information comes to light. To paraphrase English philosopher Carveth Read, it is better to be vaguely right than exactly wrong! Take a long-term view and invest sensibly for the future. Try not to worry too much about short-term forecasts, and remember, highly specific forecasts are meaningless, as they are almost always wrong.

Small sample sizes and false prophets

In his ground-breaking book *Thinking, Fast and Slow,* psychologist Daniel Kahneman invited readers to consider why some small, rural, Republican towns in America's South, West, and Midwest might've recorded the some of the highest rates of kidney cancer in the country. Perhaps it was due to the clean-living rural lifestyle, lack of pollution, and access to fresh food?

Confusingly, some small, rural, Republican towns in the South, West, and Midwest had also recorded some of the lowest rates of kidney cancer in the country. Maybe due to the challenges of living in remote regions and related poverty? The suggested explanations are nonsensical, of course. A simpler answer is that small populations are statistically more likely to produce extreme outcomes.

We see this phenomenon often enough in real estate magazines, with remote suburbs that you've never heard of featuring prominently in the 'best performing suburbs' lists. It all sounds impressive until you work out that the sample size is half a dozen transactions, and the same suburbs will likely feature in the 'worst performers' lists soon enough.

This can seem obvious, but Kahneman's research found that most of us are poor intuitive statisticians, and consequently, nowhere near as rational as we think we are.

This law (or should that be fallacy?) of small numbers extends far beyond rates of kidney cancer or real estate trends, to sports stars experiencing apparent 'hot streaks', or random results from roulette wheels. Far, far too often people place undue emphasis or reliance on the returns of small samples. Occasionally even a sample of one is enough!

Financial gurus can make their name from just one good year or open-ended prediction, though human nature dictates that they'll downplay or downright ignore their poor forecasts. It's said that forecasts tell you more about the forecaster than they do the future, and we all tend to rate commentary that confirms our underlying beliefs more highly than commentary that contradicts them.

It's usually smarter and safer to look for a proven track record over a long period of time. Wilston in Brisbane is an excellent example. Wilston is a landlocked suburb, close to good schools and transport, with all the amenities to make it a family-friendly location. As a result, it's been one of the very strongest performers in Brisbane over the past 30 years, with a consistent compounding capital growth rate of around 10 per cent per annum.

Middle Park in Melbourne is a similar high-return example, but just about any inner-ring suburb supported by rail amenity in Melbourne is a good example of consistent and attractive capital growth! Population growth and growing demand over time have virtually ensured it.

We know it can be tempting to chase boom towns and hotspots, or to follow the latest fad. It's a sad truth, though, that more often than not these strategies result in underwhelming outcomes, and sometimes catastrophic results. Warren Buffett once said that time is the friend of the great investment, and the enemy of the mediocre. When it comes to property, we cannot overemphasise this guiding principle: focus on buying the best located property you can and holding on to it for a very long period, if not forever. That's how you can benefit from the power of compound growth.

 How to beat negativity bias

Some years ago, I went to a party in Sydney where I met one of the country's best-known economic journalists. I happened to ask him whether he felt negative news articles were better received overall than those adopting a positive stance. He's a balanced and thoughtful type, and on consideration confirmed my suspicion that people, on average, rather like to hear bad news: struggling households, corruption, hypocritical politicians, and so on.

Although people often *think* they prefer good news, we're hardwired to be more responsive to negative words that are typically associated with threats. We've evolved to recall bad or adverse events with more intensity than positive episodes, because those negative experiences can help us avoid danger (whether real or perceived).

Studies by smarter folks than me have shown that in a group environment, delivering positive feedback encourages people to keep doing what they're doing well, but that some negative feedback can also be constructive insofar as it guards against complacency or stagnation. The ideal praise-to-criticism ratio has been thought to be at least 4 to 1, or possibly even higher. Yet, depending upon who we surround ourselves with and what we choose to read, the ratio of positive to negative comments and actions that we see, hear, or experience might be much lower, or even completely reversed.

Exposure to too much negativity can be contagious and leave you prone to inaction. Conversely, optimistic, positive-minded people are likely to reinforce your confidence, and inspire you to build on your strengths and fulfil your potential.

How can you overcome negativity? It's inevitable that we all experience some negativity from time to time, and sometimes it's appropriate, but here are six of the most effective ways to get the better of it:

- **Balance your fears** – be realistic about threats and negativity; live in the moment instead of projecting, and face your fears without being overawed by them. Learn to recognise negative thought patterns.
- **Positive planning** – choose constructive thoughts. Know where you're going, and don't spend too much time worrying about what others are up to.
- **Limit external negativity** – the past is the past; don't dwell on it too much. Consider going on a media fast.
- **Avoid saying, 'Yes but…'** – it's an annoying, energy-sapping phrase which you see or hear online a thousand times a day. Don't use it.
- **Get moving and take action** – exercise releases endorphins, so even a 15-minute burst of activity will makes you feel better about yourself, and in turn more likely to take positive action.

- **Change your friends** – controversial, perhaps, yet people adjust who they associate with all the time. At the very least, dialling down your exposure to draining relationships and spending more time with inspirational types will yield dividends.

Life is too short to waste on undue negativity, so aim to jettison the toxic influences! As Cate's stories earlier in this chapter illustrate so perfectly, there will always be people on hand to tell you what you're doing wrong and why!

Leverage positive influences

It's often said that you become the average of the half-dozen people you spend the most time with. That's quite likely true, because you begin to mirror the beliefs, behaviours, and practices of your peer group. If that's the case, then, as Pete just mentioned, you need to think carefully about who you spend your valuable time with.

This doesn't mean dropping less successful friends or anything like that, but it does suggest that removing toxic influences from your life and replacing them with inspiring and uplifting mentors and friends is likely to be of great benefit. This can only see you lifted to greater heights over time.

How to improve your self-esteem

We tend to be sceptical of those 'my typical day' articles and videos you see online or in lifestyle pieces. In the Instagram era, almost anyone's life can be made to look like a highlights reel; we all know that in reality, everyone has days that are less inspired or productive than others. Best not to compare yourself too readily, we would say, especially if you don't have the full picture!

In the modern world of 'direct feedback' online, we can also take negative or adverse comments too easily to heart. The fear of rejection is undoubtedly a useful evolutionary mechanism, but that usefulness probably doesn't extend to angst about snarky social media comments or daft arguments on chat forums.

Improving self-esteem is important, for if it's low, this can impact your self-image, confidence, outlook, and ultimately, your ability to succeed.

Mirroring many other *curvilinear* models, both low *and* high levels of self-esteem can be both emotionally and socially harmful, with the optimum level lying somewhere in the middle of that continuum. (In other words, it is possible to have too much of a good thing!)

If your self-esteem is lower than you'd like it to be, it's worth thinking about what the causes might be. Habits can be tough to break, but there are simple steps anyone can take to improve self-esteem. The first place to start is with Pete's list of ways to overcome negativity.

Focus on the positives about yourself, in particular, and skip the negative self-talk. People with healthy self-esteem tend not to focus too much on their mistakes: they pursue growth and improvement instead. We all make both good and 'suboptimal' choices every single day, that's human nature, so try not to beat yourself up too much. You're unique. Value yourself! Be kind to yourself!

Take time to enjoy life, too – you only get one go at it – and try to concentrate on your own game and running your own race rather than comparing yourself with others. You never know other people's true circumstances and what help they may or may not have had along the way.

Keep the snowball rolling

Hopefully by now you've started working on your property plan and thinking about how it should it be tailored to your goals, financial ability, and timeframe. To allow the compound-growth snowball to keep rolling for as long as possible to give you the maximum benefit, you also need to have some self-awareness and try to avoid self-sabotage.

We've touched on negative events that can occur that are outside our control, such as illness or divorce, but we can very effectively and quickly sabotage our own results if our wealth begins to exceed what we believe we truly deserve. This is why it's important to keep working on our self-belief, self-worth, and optimism, and reviewing our strategy and goals as we go along.

Key points in this chapter

- Optimists tend to fare better in property than pessimists.
- People are rarely rational when it comes to money and investing.
- There are always outrageous forecasts being put forward in the media. It's usually best to ignore the extreme predictions as they are rarely correct.
- Property is a long-term investment. Turn down the media commentary and noise.
- There will be setbacks along the way, but the key is how you respond to those setbacks.

6

What can go wrong?

Buy right, and your first property purchase can be the springboard for great things. We've seen that the long-term returns from property can be very attractive; you can use the equity created as a deposit to buy a second property and repeat the process again from there, or you could renovate and trade up. On the other hand, if you make a mistake with your first purchase, you may become trapped with no capital growth or even negative equity. Inevitably, every subsequent decision becomes harder from there.

The statistics show that 90 per cent of property investors never own more than two properties. That's often because they 'buy wrong'.

How do so many people get it so wrong? There are five types of buying mistakes to avoid:

1. Buying in the wrong location
2. Buying the wrong property and paying too much
3. Buying with the wrong people
4. Buying for the wrong reasons
5. Buying with inadequate planning.

Then, there are two main post-purchase errors to avoid: badly managing your investment property, and selling too soon.

Buying in the wrong location

Sometimes people buy in the wrong market. For example, during Australia's mining boom years, many investors were lured to invest in the Pilbara or the coal mining towns of Queensland, motivated by the extremely strong rental yields that were on offer for a year or two. As property prices spiralled upward, however, more properties were quickly built, leading to prices collapsing again.

Investing in these types of locations can be speculative, and you generally need good timing to make it worthwhile and to compensate for the risk. Sentiment can turn quickly, and in an illiquid market where no-one wants to buy anymore, it can be very hard to get your money back out.

When you're buying a property to live in, compromising on location can significantly impact your enjoyment of the property. This is a common mistake.

As we've already established, it's generally better to take a longer-term view and invest in landlocked markets and locations where demand is growing and there's a long and proven track record of results.

Buying the wrong property and paying too much

Cate will talk to you all day long about examples of people buying the wrong property if you let her! Location is critical, as it's the one thing you can never change about an investment, but buying the right property in those optimal locations is also important.

A fairly common mistake is paying too much for the wrong property at the peak of a market cycle. This risk can be heightened when people are buying brand-new properties, such as off-the-plan apartments or house-and-land packages. There tends to be more risk in buying a property that isn't yet built, since the end product may not match your expectations. Moreover, it tends to be more expensive to buy a brand-new property, as the developer needs to make a profit. New properties attract strong tax benefits (which we discuss later in this chapter) and are usually easier to rent out, but when you come to sell, they're no longer new and the price you achieve may be lower. The land-to-asset ratio is the technical reason for this – we go into more detail about this later in this chapter.

Statistically, more people lose money when they buy new, versus buying established property. And buying off the plan because you haven't saved an adequate deposit for an established property is a classic rookie error.

Poor quality can also be a big issue. During Australia's construction boom around a decade ago, there was a big surge in the number of high-rise units being constructed in the inner cities of Sydney, Melbourne, and Brisbane. Although median housing prices have increased over the past decade, many of these new high-rises were poorly designed and constructed and have failed to deliver as investments.

Selecting a property that is troublesome to finance is another big no-no – we go into more detail about this in chapter 10. If you commit to purchasing a property and are then unable to settle (because of, for example, wrong zoning, insufficient deposit size or the property being unacceptable to lenders as security for a loan), you'll lose your deposit.

Buying with the wrong people

There are a few different aspects to the 'wrong people' type of mistake. The first is co-purchasing with a partner who isn't Mr or Mrs Right – someone you feel isn't likely to be your partner for the long term. As upsetting as it is to recognise that a relationship is going nowhere or is breaking down, the added stress and cost associated with exiting one party from a property title, or selling the property to facilitate the split, won't improve what will already be a difficult time, and is likely to lose you money.

If you're purchasing with Mr or Mrs Right, the mistake can be to make a decision to purchase without ensuring your partner is fully on board. Nobody wants to think that a house-purchase decision could threaten a good relationship, but it can.

Advice from parents

Allowing parents to have too much input is another easy-to-make error. I can vouch for this one! By the time I had saved enough money to set my sights on property acquisition, I had someone trusted and knowledgeable in my corner – a lovely family friend called Bruce. Bruce was a real estate agent in the town that I grew up in, and he had enormous knowledge from a lifetime career in real estate. He spent time with me cutting out newspaper clippings and sharing great insights that could have helped me select a high-performance property at the time. But I didn't take his advice.

Instead, I leaned on my dad for advice. My dad was loving and protective, but not a property expert by any means. He had purchased a couple of properties in his life, and, like most dads, that was where his expertise started and stopped. To compound the issue, my dad, as a qualified accountant, was very conservative and risk-averse when it came to debt. He talked me out of a 1960s-era house in Melbourne's south-eastern suburb of Bentleigh and encouraged me to buy an off-the-plan townhouse in Mordialloc instead. The townhouse didn't outperform, but the house in Bentleigh did.

Bruce and I still catch up, and I cherish the guidance he's given me over the years in my career.

Buying an investment property for the wrong reasons

Property can be such a powerful asset class, but we've seen plenty of people make mistakes buying for the wrong reasons. It happens often! Here's the list:

- Buying for tax benefits
- Buying due to social pressure
- Buying for children
- Buying a holiday house
- Buying a home for your future self
- Buying with the idea of getting rich quick.

You may wonder what's wrong with some of these! Let's dive into why they're pitfalls.

Buying for tax benefits

Typically, a new property will deliver an optimised tax advantage. The combination of high depreciation benefits and high cashflow losses – particularly if the borrower can leverage 105 per cent of the value of the property – will ensure maximum tax rebates at the end of each financial year.

Enter the accountant who sees his or her job as only being about minimising tax. Whether it's through an accountant's bad advice or one of those slick seminars selling the virtues of new developments, many investors get caught up in their quest to save on tax. They forget that *making a loss* is what generates tax benefits – and often they create some sizable losses and/or lost opportunities for themselves, underestimating the lost capital growth that a better-quality asset could have generated for them over time.

While depreciation helps with cashflow, it should never be the reason for investing in property. Negative gearing and investor tax benefits are sometimes featured heavily in the media, so let's put perspective around the issue. After all, why do most investors choose property as an asset class? Not just for the tax breaks!

Depreciation

In a property-investment context, depreciation is a decrease in value of the property and/or its fixtures and fittings due to age and wear and tear.

 ### Depreciation and land-to-asset value

All too often, I meet investors who have a sad tale about the limited value growth of their brand-new or newly refurbished apartment. Whether it be an apartment in Melbourne's Docklands, an outer-ring Sydney refurbishment or a southern Queensland coastal off-the-plan development, the stories have a lot in common. Many purchasers find themselves making a loss when they sell their property within a few years of the initial purchase.

Yet every week, without fail, I speak to prospective investors who wish to purchase investment properties with high depreciation benefits. Likewise, my business gets targeted by marketing groups offering lucrative commissions for their brand-new, off-the-plan stock. Explaining that we don't target brand-new builds comes as a shock to some of these enquirers, but the reason is simple: when depreciation is high, the property is often making a loss.

This may seem like simple logic, but it is quite challenging to explain to someone who either promotes brand-new properties for a living or tells their clients to target cashflow savings for accountancy reasons. I recall a conversation I once had with a client's accountant after their advice clashed with my property investment advice. The accountant told me, 'Cate, my job is to save them tax'. I replied, 'No, *our* job is to help them build wealth'.

To illustrate why depreciation should never be a reason to buy an investment property, here are the three important attributes that investors should be focusing on:

1. Long-term, sustained capital growth
2. Reliable and consistent rental yield
3. Tight vacancy rates.

There is no amount of depreciation benefit that can make up for any of these three attributes underperforming. If the property is difficult to rent out – due to either an oversupply of similar properties in the area or a limited tenant pool – the depreciation will only help the cashflow so much.

Eventually, if the holding costs are too great, the investor will need to sell the property – even if they haven't held it long enough for the capital growth to be positive. In other words, if the property is worth less than what they originally paid for it, they will incur a loss. When purchase and selling costs are added to this, the whole exercise becomes even more painful.

Not all brand-new and off-the-plan properties lose value immediately after purchase, but most do. The reason for this is that the **land-to-asset ratio** is too low. The land-to-asset ratio is simply the value of the land purchased relative to the value of the dwelling on that land. If the land component is worth under 50 per cent of the overall purchase price – meaning that the dwelling is worth more than the land – this is problematic. In this situation, the rate of depreciation of the dwelling can easily be greater than the rate of appreciation of the land component.

Sure, the investor may enjoy the depreciation benefit as a tax rebate in July, but what's the point of sustaining out-of-pocket costs, carrying risk, and wasting mental energy on a property that's worth less a few years later? Surely a different type of purchase with a more likely return on investment is a better idea.

Here's an example. A block of apartments in Yarraville in Melbourne's inner west was sold off the plan in 2012, and construction was finalised in the two years following. The sales dates and results shown in table 6.1 are for one apartment in the block, with the initial purchase in April of that year.

Table 6.1: sales dates and results for an apartment in Yarraville

Sold date	Sale price
12 April 2012	$509,000
25 May 2016	$491,000
26 May 2018	$492,000

It could be argued that the original purchaser paid a premium price (and this often happens when developers employ marketers to sell), but put simply, the dwelling's depreciation outstripped the land component's appreciation during their period of ownership.

Depreciation amounts vary depending on the quantity surveyor's determination of the plant, equipment, and building value. However, a rough guide for this apartment would have potentially been around the $10,000 mark for year 1 and then diminishing incrementally year after year. Had this investor bought a property with higher capital growth prospects, they'd have forfeited this attractive depreciation incentive, but they would most likely have experienced some capital growth instead of losses. So, not only was the property costing them in out-of-pocket cashflow, but it also cost them in lost opportunity.

Cate always reminds her clients that depreciation tax benefits aren't a bad thing, but they are merely a benefit, not a reason to invest.

Poor-performing properties in high-performing suburbs

In many popular inner-ring areas where amenities, public transport, lifestyle, and desirability reign, certain blocks can perform counter to other properties in the same suburb. These poor-performing investments are heartbreakers for investors, and it's mainly due to depreciation and low land-to-asset ratio. Let's dive into a little more detail using one of my client's purchases as a case study.

In 2016, I bid at auction on a beautifully converted two-bedroom, two-bathroom warehouse apartment with an enclosed balcony in Kensington. Its location – just 3 kilometres from the CBD, with easy access to shops, stations and arterials – was just one of the drawcards for my buyer. The secure block, car space on the title, and separate storage unit on offer delivered on just about every criterion she had. Units in the suburb had eclipsed 6 per cent growth over the preceding 12 months – so the findings of my research came as a bit of a surprise.

The previous owners had paid $655,000 back in 2010, when the original warehouse block was stripped, rebuilt, and released by a developer. At the time, all the other sales in the block were quite comparable, with sales of two-bedroom units sitting between $650,000 and $720,000. Buyers back in late 2009 and into 2010 had clearly bought with enthusiasm, whether the purpose of their purchase was occupation or investment.

So, why did my comparable sales analysis indicate that a lesser figure would likely result some six years later?

The obvious consideration is that perhaps the vendor overpaid at the time their initial purchase, but in fact this was not the reason. Comparable sales evidence of all other two-bedroom dwellings within the same complex indicated that the problem was consistent across all properties and for all owners.

Nobody ever purchases property and anticipates that over a six-year period they will sustain a capital loss. In fact, a common property misconception is that property values double every seven years. Yet, units in this complex, in this dynamic, popular, and enviable suburb, were transacting at a loss.

Was it just that buyers had purchased at a market peak back in 2010? This was almost certainly a factor, but the Kensington market had not only recovered since then but had continued to grow significantly beyond the highs of that 2010 peak.

Post-settlement depreciation was the key factor in the negative capital growth this apartment sustained.

The development would have sparked interest back in 2009 when the available 'warehouse conversions' were on offer to the public. Quality finishes, generous spaces, great fixtures and fittings, and a high depreciation schedule would have enticed many buyers to consider opting in. Many investors get excited about new developments and refurbishments, particularly when hefty tax deductions through depreciation may be on offer. As I touched on earlier, we often have clients coming to us with instructions from their accountant to pursue a new property for tax-saving reasons.

What investors often forget is that depreciation means *losing value.* It's only acceptable for a dwelling to lose value if the land it sits on is growing at a strong enough rate to offset the rate of the depreciation.

In an apartment block like this, it's more difficult to determine the exact land ownership percentage that can be allocated to one owner. Common areas in strata developments are often considered to be 'undivided and equally shared' among residents, but for the purposes of calculating the 'relative share' of the land value, apartments of different sizes may be determined to have unequal ownership of the land. It varies between complexes.

However, the relative land ownership per resident back in 2009 in terms of land value would have been distinctly lower than the value of their dwelling. After all, the brand-new fittings and fixtures, quality build, and exciting interiors had zero depreciation. They had never been used. Buying one of these apartments was just like driving a car with zero kilometres on the odometer out of the lot.

From the moment of settlement, the calculated rate of depreciation would have been quite high, and any investors in the block would presumably have made some decent tax savings. But depreciation is an inverse-compounding situation: as the years go by, the tax write-downs diminish year on year until one day, they're negligible.

Sadly for the first owner, in the case of this property, the first five years of ownership saw the property diminish in value while depreciation was running high.

Land-to-asset ratio underpins so much of our decision-making as advocates and investment property advisors, and it's always disappointing to see situations like this where vendors could have invested their savings differently, but instead have sustained a market loss.

For our buyer, though, who secured the property for $631,000 under auction, her timing probably couldn't have been better. With the slowdown in the rate of the apartment's depreciation, and with ever-popular Kensington's land values increasing, the block had just turned the corner in terms of capital growth. Her property is still glossy and fabulous, but the key for her is that the land-to-asset ratio is now at a much healthier percentage.

The most valuable tip I can share on this matter is to always aim for a land-to-asset ratio of greater than 50 per cent.

Nobody likes to pay tax, but buying an underperforming asset (or worse still, an asset that loses value and is tough to rent out) is a terrible idea.

Social pressure

Succumbing to peer group competition is as serious a mistake as chasing tax benefits when it comes to acquiring an investment property. From pilots who chat in the cockpit to anaesthetists who chat while watching a patient's vital signs, barbecue buddies who chat over beer to office workers chatting around the water-cooler, many investors decide to jump onto a bandwagon for social status or due to a secret fear that their friends could amass wealth and leave them in their wake.

Deciding to invest when a success story has influenced you is one thing, but deciding to invest because you're feeling competitive is never a good idea.

Furthermore, copying a friend's purchase strategy is fraught with danger. Property investment approaches are never 'one-size-fits-all', because so many variables determine the most fitting strategy. Which strategy is right for you depends on your:

- retirement income goals
- investments in other asset classes that will contribute to retirement income
- debt retirement plans (your plans for how to pay off loans)
- time until retirement
- risk profile
- current commitments
- current income
- personal household cashflow
- ability to renovate or actively work on the property
- interest in developing, subdividing, or altering the property
- borrowing capacity and lending constraints.

What may work for your friend may clash with your own personal financial situation and future goals. Imagine treading in your friend's footsteps and committing to a similar property to theirs, only to find that your out-of-pocket monthly contribution starts to eat into your lifestyle?

Or, on the flip side, say you purchase a moderately performing asset that is better suited to your friend's personal cashflow situation, only to discover that you could have purchased a superior performing asset and generated a significantly stronger equity position in the following ten years?

Doing it for the kids

So many well-meaning parents buy property with their children in mind. Some plot out a strategy to secure little Johnny a home near a university; others like to ensure that they'll have their kids just around the corner from them. Those who are sensitive to increasing house prices love the idea of securing a position on the property ladder for their children. We've met plenty of parents who have masterminded a plan for their toddler, and even a few who had unborn children in mind.

The reality is that we don't know where our children's lives will take them, when they will wish to inhabit their own home, how they'll dream of doing it, and more importantly, what we're stealing from them when we fulfil a goal that could have been important for them to set and achieve on their own.

Will little Johnny grow up and want to live in the same neighbourhood as you? Could his life take him abroad? Could he determine that his investment portfolio is more suited to liquid assets? Could he attract opportunistic people over the course of his life because his parents handed him a house on a platter? Buying a home for a child can be a drama in disguise for those parents who don't think through the possible ramifications.

There *are* ways to help children onto the property ladder – but allowing them to set their own goals in this area can make the difference between a grateful child and an entitled one.

Then, for example, parents who consider buying a unit 'in town' for a university undergraduate child may not have done their homework on the ideal tenant. An 18- to 22-year-old isn't the obvious choice if you want a stable, neat tenant who lives a quiet lifestyle and maintains a property well. Many don't clean particularly well, plenty invite partners (so a two-bedroom apartment becomes a four-person household, with double-strength wear and tear), and neighbourly upset can strike when parties are held.

Not all undergraduates are troublesome tenants, but in a sea of applicants that also includes professional and mature tenants, most property managers would opt for the latter if given the choice. To compound the risk, the locations and dwelling types of university-centric property may not deliver the strong capital growth that could be found elsewhere.

There are various ways that parents can help their children get into property, and everyone's situation, risk profile, and approach is unique. Options include gifting deposits, providing family pledge loans, purchasing property as joint tenants or tenants-in-common, earmarking properties in trusts for future gifts, and so on. One thing that these all have in common, however, is the requirement for legal advice or statutory declarations.

This is for good reason: helping loved ones financially can carry risk, and parents need to fully understand the scope of their assistance and the implications going forward. In situations where shared responsibility ensues, you want to know that your children will cope with the responsibility and benefit from it.

You never want, for example, a gift to create turmoil or result in land in the wrong hands in future years. Legal advice is important when considering the arrangement itself, the estate planning associated with the property and the responsibility each party is taking on.

Pete and his wife chose to aid their twenty-something son in selecting a suitable rental property and assisted him with his application and bond.

 Helping my stepson onto the property ladder

In 2015, I collaborated with my then 21-year-old stepson to help him onto the property ladder. Rob was still living at home with his mum, work was an easy commute, and he had no reason to consider buying his own home. Having grown up around property investment, though, he knew that a disciplined savings plan and investing early were ideas to canvass with us.

My husband and I decided with Rob what arrangement would work for us. Rob was an apprentice carpenter at the time, and while he didn't have remarkable savings, he did have remarkable energy and ability to renovate. If we could fund the 10 per cent deposit, he could renovate the house.

At the time, his apprentice wages couldn't have easily covered a cashflow shortfall, and while we were excited to see him start his personal wealth journey, we didn't want to pay for a cashflow shortfall either. This meant that we had to target a property exhibiting stronger rental returns than normal.

I identified three-bedroom, structurally sound houses on compact and subdivided blocks in Melbourne as ideal contenders. I also wanted to ensure that the capital growth prospects would reward him, so I focused on the gentrifying suburbs in the west middle-ring as close to rail amenity as my budget would allow. Sunshine and Albion had already exhibited substantial growth and change, and while I had no doubt that residential investment in this pocket would continue to flourish, we'd been priced out by the recent growth.

Ideally, I needed to find a property that could provide a gross rental yield well above 4 per cent and preferably around 4.5 per cent. To meet our cashflow target (a minimal 'out-of-pocket' contribution each month), I had worked out that a standard, renovated three-bedroom brick home in the area typically rented for $360 per week, and hence I had a budget of around $400,000 to work with.

My calls to agents worked well. We had a few options to choose from, but it was a triple-fronted brick house on 307 square metres in Sunshine West that seemed to fit the brief. It was presented well, partially renovated, and screaming out for a new bathroom, laundry, and landscaping.

We secured the property for $405,000 in September 2015.

Our 50/50 tenants-in-common arrangement with Rob meant that he owned his half-share, and his labour over the January break added significant value to the property.

Three years on, our second tenant was residing in the property. It was a relatively seamless period of low-maintenance, consistent rental income and attractive tax returns for Rob. The biggest benefit for him has been the capital growth.

He's been happy to accept that the property is purely an investment, and a 'buy and hold' purchase. It's not to be inhabited by him, and its equity is not to be accessed for anything other than future property purchases or business investment. We all agreed on this strategy at commencement.

At 23, Rob had already generated enough equity to take on a second project. That first purchase has proven to be a great foundation for his subsequent investments, and we're very happy with the arrangement and proud of him.

I see parents assisting their children on a regular basis, whether it's providing moral support at opens and auctions or financial contributions. Whatever the method that works for each family, there are ways that children can be helped in property. And while housing affordability (or the lack thereof) for our young people gets a lot of media attention, thinking outside the box, as we did with Rob, might provide a different solution. They don't have to buy where they want to live.

Note that it's important, of course, to check whether there are first-homebuyer concessions or grants available in the state you're intending to purchase in. The rules are changeable, so it's always worth double-checking.

Buying a holiday house

Every January, without fail, Cate fields questions from new and past clients about her thoughts on their holiday-house acquisition ideas, and every year she learns more about why this is such a well-trodden path. The reasons are always emotional and never, ever pragmatic. But when is it OK for emotion to rule? When is a holiday house a good idea?

Because this is such an emotional topic, we're going to try to answer thoughtfully. For so many people, the mere idea of a holiday house is driven by a strong force, whether it be the dream to gather family and create memories, to escape the daily grind, to give a sense of relaxation, or to add a new and happy dimension to their lifestyle.

The reality is, however, that a holiday house is not an asset in the same sense that a pure investment property is. A pure investment should be considered on financial, timing, and practicality measures. Annual returns, costs of holding, borrowing capacity, long-term growth, target tenants, and debt retirement strategy are all facets to tick off the list when buying an investment property.

As soon as personal use creeps into the equation, that purity of vision is no more, and the waters start to get murky.

So many investors approach investing with personal use in mind, whether it be, 'One day I might downsize into this unit' or 'My kids might live in it when they go to university'. As soon as a personal-use criterion forms part of the brief, it can overshadow choosing the most suitable areas and dwelling types for the investor's financial goals.

Holiday homes are often much more debilitating to an investor's financial strategy than a unit that they 'may' move into one day; they present significant challenges. Here are some of the most common:

- The owner usually wants to stay in the property when the rental potential is at its highest (that is, when the property is most in demand and can be let for the highest price – during the Christmas break, for example).
- Holiday properties are tough to let during down times without significant management, laundry, and cleaning costs.

- A long-term residential tenancy may not be all that suitable for the property, and so the tenants may be less desirable.
- Tax benefits will likely be eroded or completely negated if the property is for personal use.
- The upkeep of the property can become draining – owners can feel their weekends at the property are spent maintaining or cleaning it.
- Conflict can arise when family members feel that the use or costs of the property are not shared equally.
- Rates, maintenance, land tax, and insurances are often heftier than anticipated and the viability of holding the property can be questioned.

These points can all be upsetting for potential holiday-home owners, but there are two other points which they often neglect to answer that could be vital to the decision-making process:

1. Is the property likely to outperform a similarly priced alternative property in the capital growth stakes? Or, could a different, more pragmatic decision to invest enable you to buy your coastal or country dream home in years to come? Cate has seen some happy and successful holiday-house stories, but she's seen plenty of sad stories too. Holiday hotspots can be volatile in terms of price, and there's nothing more deflating for an investor than selling for a loss.
2. If you forecast the expenditure and out-of-pocket costs associated with buying a pure investment property and simply leasing a regular holiday rental each year, would you be better off financially compared to owning your own holiday house? The reality is that we only get one life, and life is meant for living. It's worth considering whether provisioning some money every year to rent out someone *else's* holiday house would make more sense and create less stress.

Genuine emotional reasons can be solid, but if the property will cause stress, upset, or financial strain, or set back your retirement or wealth-creation plans, the purchase really does deserve caution. The flow chart shown in figure 6.1 (as basic as it seems) is what Cate often draws in her notebook when she's talking to someone about whether a holiday house is a good idea for them.

Figure 6.1: is buying a holiday house a good idea?

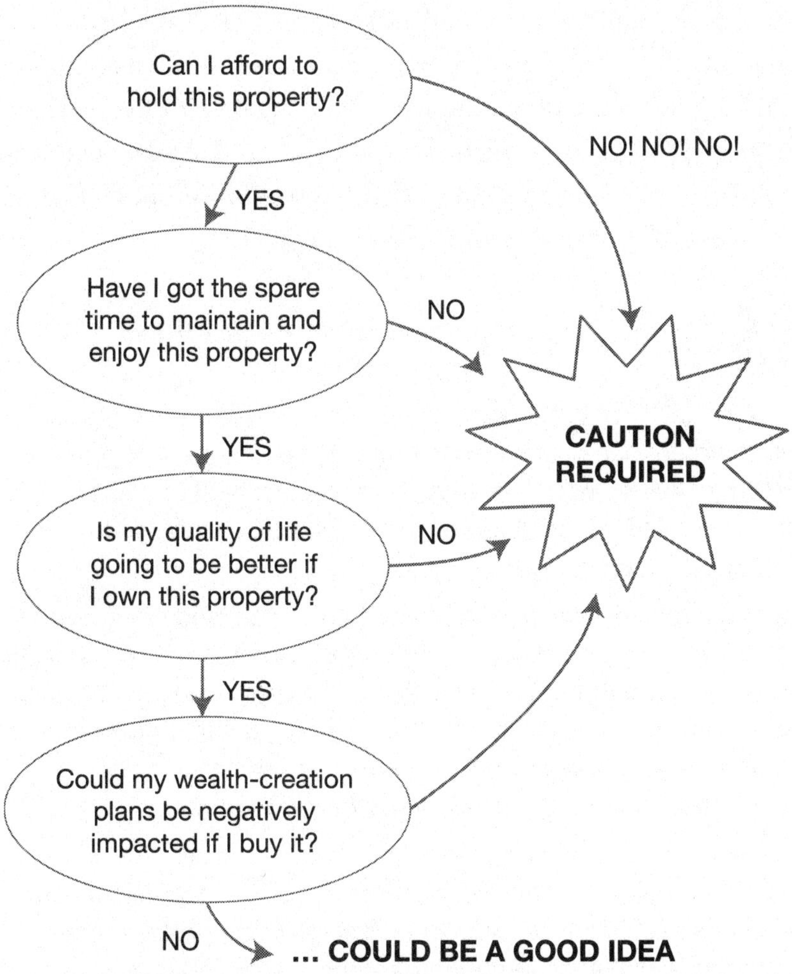

January often tugs at our heartstrings and reminds us of beautiful family times and friendship experiences, but a holiday house is more than just a few free weekends away – it's a serious financial decision.

Purchasing a home for your future self

Buyers who are purchasing for their future use as opposed to *now* or *soon* are taking a gamble. Things change, opportunities present themselves, and desires change as we move through life – envisaging where you might be more than about three years into the future is fraught with risk. You could purchase a 'future home' that's impractical for you now, only to find when you reach that forecast future, the property is far from what you want and need. And all that time, you may have been servicing a negative-cashflow property that was not an effective or high-scoring investment.

 My misguided future-self home purchase

I was struck by a 'What was I thinking?' moment myself after a 'future home' purchase in a different state over a decade ago. It seemed like a good idea at the time, but my husband and I compromised our capital-growth strategy by wrongly predicting our family's future needs.

We had a special affinity with Hobart, Tasmania, and after several long weekend trips down to the beautiful maritime city, we decided we'd like to live there permanently. We had jobs in Melbourne and a tiny baby in tow, and almost all our friends, family, networks and contacts were in Melbourne. Our work opportunities in Hobart were limited at best. We hadn't thought this through!

We knew that an imminent move was out of the question and settled on a seven- to ten-year horizon for our Hobart relocation. We interviewed local schools and formulated our property criteria list with gusto. We targeted central Hobart, with aspirations of easy walks into town, heritage character surrounds, and an ample number of bedrooms to welcome friends and family. And we found a gorgeous four-bedroom beauty in postcode 7000 for $560,000 (*Welona*, mentioned in chapter 5).

Life evolved for us, though. I established my career doing what I love in Melbourne, and our family and friends are an important part of our life here. Moving to Hobart is not feasible for us, nor would I want to leave my home city now. While our red-brick house with Hobart city views is beautiful, we are not likely to ever live in it. It has performed well in terms of capital growth and increased rental return, but it hasn't outperformed a well-located period house in Melbourne.

The property is probably worth around $1.2 million in today's market. Had we purchased a similar property in Melbourne at that time instead, our $560,000 spend would have translated into a stronger current value. For example, a property within easy walk of Yarraville village sold at the same time for a very similar price, boasting beautiful internal features and offering the same accommodation and living spaces as our $560,000 Hobart acquisition. It sold in May 2018 for $1.625 million.

Our limited insight into our own future needs and the viability of our Tasmania move cost us in lost opportunity.

However, not all future dreams come at a material cost, and not all are a bad idea. Recognising that your needs will change and that your desired lifestyle will evolve is important, and some future plans (and the criteria that result) are clever. Buying a larger house for a growing family is one of the most common things couples do to future-proof their purchase.

Focusing on mobility options and ease of maintenance is also important for those who wish to grow old in their own home. And considering commute times has worked well for many a buyer to maximise precious time with loved ones at home when a significant job change is on the horizon.

Future-proofing a home like this can save you significant cost and stress if you plan well, consider the likelihood of the change, factor in the cost to reverse your decision, and assess its viability.

Some of the more challenging future-based ideals, though, can result in financial loss, lost opportunity and/or significant 'trading' costs (such as stamp duty and agent's selling fees) when the plans don't come to fruition. They include:

· purchasing a holiday house when life is too busy to maintain or enjoy it

· making a tree-change or sea-change without careful consideration

· buying city units for student-children before their academic options are clear

· pursuing 'downsizer ideals' long before retirement.

If any of these apply to you, ask yourself whether you should wait, keep saving, and consider investing your money elsewhere for the time being – whether into an investment property or a conservative, liquid asset such as blue-chip shares, bonds or term deposits.

Buying with the idea of getting rich quick

Many investors hold the false belief that property delivers fast profits. Unfortunately, idealistic consumers pay exorbitant amounts each year on property seminars, fast-profit gurus and formulae that are either doomed from the start or carry extraordinarily high risk.

The reality is that property is generally not an asset class that can make people wealthy in a short space of time. Despite the media hype about record growth years in specific areas, we can't expect property performance to replicate these years, nor can we expect growth to be linear.

Trading in a short timeframe is a huge risk for any Australian property investor, especially when combined with Australian acquisition, holding, and divestment (selling) costs, which include the following:

- **Stamp duty.** Also called 'transfer duty', 'land transfer duty' and 'conveyance duty', this is paid by purchasers. In Australia, stamp duty is relatively expensive. Rates vary between different states and territories; at time of writing, Victoria was the costliest, charging between 1.4 per cent and 6 per cent on a sliding scale depending on the value of the property. Each state also has its own set of stamp duty waivers, exemptions and concessions, but these are limited and often one-time use.

- **Legal costs.** These include conveyancing fees for services like preparing or reviewing the contract of sale, payable by either the buyer or seller.

- **Land tax.** Investors need to factor in that they will be paying land tax during their period of ownership.

- **Capital gains tax.** This may need to be paid upon the sale of a property.

- **Selling costs.** These include real estate agents' fees (typically between 1.5 to 3 per cent of the sale price) and the cost of marketing a property for sale, which could be very low for just an online search-engine listing, or as high as tens of thousands of dollars for ads in printed media. People who choose to enhance their property's appeal with professional interior-design help will also incur styling costs.

- **Lender fees.** Lenders may charge establishment or exit fees.

These costs can make it difficult to get a fast profit out of property. For all those who manage to make a tidy profit, plenty of traders don't!

In fact, selling a property after less than three years of ownership is overwhelmingly likely to result in an overall loss. We suggest holding property for five years as an absolute minimum – in a positively trending capital city, it's likely you'll recover your purchase costs within this timeframe. Adopting such a short-term approach is dangerous, however, as the reasons for an unforeseen sale are numerous; for example:

- An unwillingness to retain the property as an investment if short-term needs change
- The need to release capital for a subsequent purchase
- A requirement to sell as a result of visa status.

If taking risks and playing your odds is your thing, maybe putting it all on black at the casino is a better option? Property investment is a long game and deserves commitment, patience, and a pragmatic approach.

We believe that property-investment decisions should be based on a long-term 'buy and hold' principle, provided that consistent and sustainable growth drivers are present. As a buyer, if you know your purchase is only for the short term, it would be wise to consider alternative investments.

Buying with inadequate planning

We go into planning in much more detail in chapter 10. Suffice it to say here that purchasing property on a whim – like you're choosing a pair of shoes – isn't a great idea. Without a good plan and an endgame, you could end up:

- not conducting adequate due diligence
- not considering your tolerance, desired involvement, and risk profile
- procrastinating or avoiding good opportunities for silly reasons

- compromising on your must-haves – or, worse still, not formulating any to start with
- ignoring cashflow.

Selling too soon

A common post-purchase mistake is selling too soon in order to 'lock in' gains. This often leads to regret further down the track, especially in landlocked city suburbs. Pete once had a lovely old client whose grandfather had sold a house in Darling Point for £50,000 back in the 1950s, which was considered a huge sum of money at the time. Fast-forward to today, however, and the block would be worth more than $30 million!

That's an extreme example, of course, but it's very common for people who sell well-located property to regret it later.

 The importance of smart loan structuring

I didn't understand loan structuring very well when I was young, and I should have made the effort to. Instead, I naively went straight to the bank and let the lending consultants pluck a loan product off the shelf and sign me up. I didn't take offset accounts into consideration, nor did I think about future tax-deductibility options.

My naivety was silly, and I paid a price for it. I not only left money on the table, but I also reduced my ability to convert good properties I'd owner-occupied into investments, because I only understood one way to unlock capital growth gains: selling. Instead of refinancing loans to access equity, I sold good properties to unlock my gains. I then leapfrogged into a subsequent purchase, and so on. It took me four ownership cycles to discover the merits of a good strategic mortgage broker and smart loan structuring.

I haven't made that mistake since, and my husband and I haven't sold good properties we've previously lived in. What's more, we haven't lost future tax benefits either. We've preserved our loan balances on investments, channelled our surplus income into offset accounts and sensibly navigated our portfolio cashflows.

We mentioned the FIRE approach ('Financial Independence Retire Early') back in chapter 2, and how to calculate how much money is enough for you to live a life that aligns with your purpose. However, some neuroscientists argue that the right time to retire is… never! Why? Because idle time spent with no purpose can lead to unhappiness.

This may be true, which is why so few people genuinely retire early. We've found that one of the things property wealth can give you, however, is the flexibility to choose what to do with your time, rather than being tied to any particular job or career.

There is a potential trap here. Some people will never have 'enough'.

Be careful if you recognise this trait in yourself, because it may mean you have a tendency to take high risks in order to get ahead. Over a long enough time horizon, this approach can undo everything – and often, the use of leverage is to blame.

Charlie Munger once said that 'ladies, liquor, or leverage' are the only three ways to go bust. Warren Buffett quipped that Munger only added the first two because they began with 'l' – implying that that the only way people really go bust is through leverage, or over-extending themselves.

As a case in point, in the early 1970s investment manager Rick Guerin was spoken of in the same breath as Buffett and Munger and had partnered with them on various projects. But Guerin faded into obscurity in the 1980s. Why?

Reportedly, the reason was that Rick Guerin was in a hurry to become super-wealthy and therefore used huge-margin loans to accelerate his results. By contrast, Buffett has noted that he and Charlie knew they were going to be rich, so they weren't in a hurry. When the market declined in 1973 and 1974, Guerin's excessive leverage led to a catastrophic wipe-out for him. Although he recovered to some degree in the following years, he was forced to sell his Berkshire stock to Buffett at $40 per share to pay back his debts. At the time of writing, the Berkshire share price is about ten times that amount.

This took place long before Betfair accounts and Bitcoin existed, which got Pete thinking about this in a bit more detail. A ramble through the myriad ways in which people become insolvent – investing in pyramid schemes, backing music tours, being sued, selling drugs, having affairs, having unexpected illnesses, and wasting inheritance windfalls, to name a few – saw some common themes emerge. There may be some crossover between the categories, but he came up with six key causes of people going broke:

1. **Bad relationships**, including with friends who give poor advice

2. **Materialism**, which is an unfulfilling game that can never truly be won (so, if you're prone to 'keeping up with the Joneses', beware)

3. **Lack of knowledge** about scams, investing, or business practice

4. **Excessive leverage**, which can take a range of forms, but most often refers to debt

5. **Ruinous bets,** including those made by budding real estate investors, which are also generally a debt issue

6. **Addictions**, which can include gambling (as above), but can take numerous other chemical or behavioural forms, from substance abuse to shopping. How do you avoid addictions? A glib response might be, 'Don't engage with vices in the first place', but qualified psychotherapists suggest combining abstinence with treating the psychological dependence and investigating the root cause of the destructive behaviour.

Aiming high safely

Thinking big is a worthy outlook – aim for the stars then maybe land on the moon, and all that – but it's not so ideal if you burn up on the journey. Here, then, are four ways to manage risk:

1. **Manage debt.** Ignorance is not bliss when it comes to financial obligations! Be familiar with the lender(s), terms, and repayment status of your liabilities.
2. **Stop worrying what others think.** Spending on stuff that isn't really needed rarely helps the cause, so don't go broke trying to look rich.
3. **Read widely.** Educate yourself. Try to challenge your own preconceptions.
4. **Diversify.** The future is far less predictable than we tend to think, so all your eggs should not be in one basket.

Ultimately, it falls to you to manage the risks. After all, no one cares about your money more than you do.

Key points in this chapter

- Property success is fundamentally simple, yet we see people coming unstuck all the time.
- To stay alive as an investor for the long term, you need to manage risk.
- 'Land appreciates, buildings depreciate.' Aim to buy properties with a strong land-to-asset ratio of at least 50 per cent.
- Get-rich-quick schemes rarely work anywhere, and this is particularly true in property.
- If you fail to plan, you have a plan to fail.

7

Getting stuck into it

In a sense, building wealth is very simple. There are only four steps that you need to be able to follow:

1. Spend less than you earn.
2. Invest the difference.
3. Reinvest the gains.
4. Protect your wealth.

And yet, when you look at most people's financial statements, what do you see? Each time their income goes up, so too do their lifestyle expenses. They take out debts for the things they can't afford: higher education, cars, whitegoods, furniture, weddings, honeymoons, holidays, and so on. Their consumer debts mean that compound growth is working in reverse. (Well, it's still working, but for the lender.) Very often, they experience a major setback somewhere along the journey when life gets in the way.

In other words, most people never really get past step 1. To some degree, it doesn't matter if you're billionaire Jeff Bezos or a youngster starting out on your journey – the principles of wealth creation are exactly the same. If you spend everything you earn, it's very hard to get ahead.

This is why building a saving habit is important. Remember Charlie Munger's advice to do whatever it takes to save your first US$100,000 – to move heaven and earth to get that first pool of capital working for you? Accumulating that US$100,000 from a standing start, he said, is the hardest part of building wealth. The dollar figure might be different today, but the principle is still very important.

Saving that first pool of money can indeed be hard work – but the good news is, once you start investing, you reach a tipping point (see figure 7.1). After that, you start gathering momentum and things get a lot easier.

Figure 7.1: the tipping point

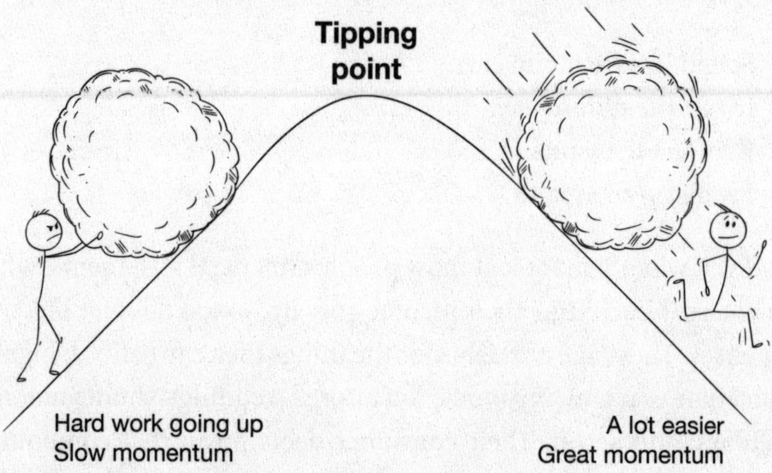

Tipping point

Hard work going up
Slow momentum

A lot easier
Great momentum

Creating a savings habit

We probably all know of people who can't save and what happens to them financially over time. It's tough! They often spend 200 hours per month at work, pay their tax, and the rest just gets... spent.

The scary thing is that we know people who earn $50,000, or $100,000, or even $500,000 per annum, and the story is the same.

There's no question that it's very hard to save your way to wealth. The government snaffles up to half of your income in tax before you can even lay your hands on it, and inflation and expenditure tend to take care of most of the rest. That being said, saving a deposit to get started in property can be critical. We know how hard it is, because we've both been through the process on multiple occasions.

 Cate's approach

As my dad said, I was 'a good little saver' as a kid, and I had a great work ethic. I got my first official job at age 14 (after working in Dad's hi-fi shop for a measly $5 per day). The local beach café was always bustling, and I'd been buying six lemonade icy poles there each weekend for my brothers, cousins, and Dad for years.

I hand-wrote a letter and nervously handed it to the owner one afternoon; she smiled briefly, turned around, bent down into a drawer, and then tossed me an apron.

I was worth $7 an hour at the Sorrento Aquarium Café, and I could hardly believe my earning power at that tender age. My poor dad lost his cheap labour, but my social confidence flourished in that job, as did my count of good workmates.

I saved the lion's share of my earnings and said yes to every available shift. Our school bank (run at lunchtime on a Friday by some older volunteer kids and the maths teacher) paid an annual interest rate of 11 per cent on savings. My parents were struggling with a hefty mortgage with horrendously high interest rates, but the cash rate certainly supported those with good term deposits. By the time I was 16 I had over $3000 saved. At the time, my savings regime was all about buying my first car, but the journey was valuable, and in hindsight, I recognise two important considerations that set me on my way.

First, I liked the compounding effect of the interest returns. Today, term deposits don't offer the same rich benefit to cash savers, but other investing methods do, and it was that 11 per cent, calculated daily, that was a bit of a thrill to me back in the day. I could make $330 per year while I was sleeping, all just by not withdrawing any of my savings.

Second, I chose a job that wasn't horrible. Going to work in the café on a busy Saturday and Sunday didn't feel like a terrible sacrifice at all. I got to work hard with my work buddies, and we were a cohesive team, with ovens running, and bacon and eggs always on the go. I was almost always assigned the role of managing the till and the orders because I was good at maths, friendly under pressure and (obviously) honest. By the time I was approaching senior school, I had keys to the café and would either open early or close late, bagging up the takings and placing orders for the following day. In that role I was trusted and had a lot of fun.

The best jobs don't feel like work. Funnily enough, I was working too hard to have time to spend the money. I appreciated the forced savings which resulted from this, though. Many of my schoolmates were spending all their money on concerts, going out, takeaway food, dates with boys and all the rest. I was having a whale of a time with my workmates at the café after closing instead. We had access to boats and floating aqua-bikes, and we hung out at each other's houses too.

I loved my days in the café – in fact, I cried when I had to resign to leave for university in the city. By the time I got to university, I wanted a similar job – where the crew was fun, the work was constant (time goes fast when you're busy), and the earning potential was good. Night shift in the Coles deli was my next opportunity to earn. The penalty rates were amazing at night, and particularly over weekends. It was a bit of a sacrifice, because Saturday night for a university student is meant to be more fun than slicing ham and cleaning chicken rotisseries, but I liked the income.

Even after my weekly expenses, I had considerable savings banked. After a year of working, with a savings balance of over

$15,000, I set myself a goal to save a house deposit of 20 per cent by the time I finished my third year. I tracked local auction results and kept an eye on asking prices. Things weren't online then like they are now, so I had a lot of clippings and cut-outs, and I annoyed real estate agents by calling and asking what certain properties had sold for. I look back now and recognise that doing what I was doing kept my ambition of home-ownership alive, and enabled me to track my progress against my goal.

That goal did mean that I had to say no to a lot of fun things, though. Outings were enjoyed on a budget. Dinners and movies were always shop-a-docket, tight-arse-Tuesday deals, or entertainment book tear-outs. If it wasn't cheap, I wasn't going.

I didn't really drink much in my university years, but if I did, it was cheap stuff – boxes of wine, cheap mixers… but that isn't unusual for university students. Our chemistry ball was held in one of the labs, and the senior students thought it was a novel idea to drink cocktails out of large test tubes. When we ran out of fresh test tubes, instead of washing and drying them, we raided the first-year lab and used their test tubes. Goodness knows what traces of stuff we ingested! But it was fun, and so very cheap. Student life is just that.

Being able to run a tight budget and manage it weekly was how I saved a deposit for a house before I finished university. Learning to sew, learning to cook, not wasting energy on heating and cooling, and saying yes to every shift I could manage were my best saving secrets!

 Pete's approach

When I was in my twenties, it felt impossible not to go out and socialise after work. Friday nights, Saturdays, and Sundays were for the pub, and quite often other nights of the week as well!

My wife Heather bought her first property at 21, and I bought my own first place in Bondi in Sydney. Some capital growth from that allowed us to use equity towards another investment property in Sydney. At that point we'd reached a bit of a dead end, and we realised that if we were going to keep moving forward, we'd need to save deposits for the next few properties in our portfolio.

I've never been one for going into great detail (which maybe shows why I was never going to be the world's best accountant!), and I knew that carefully drawing up a budget with expense categories wasn't going to work for us. Instead, we had to identify the big-ticket expense items that might prevent us from saving the deposits we wanted. For us they were international travel, cars, and in particular, socialising (that is, the pub!).

We chose to forego having an international holiday in favour of a couple of local holidays in New South Wales. We also used a car-sharing service for a year, since we lived at Pyrmont within walking distance of Sydney city. The car-sharing was a so-so experience, to be honest, but it served its purpose.

By far the hardest thing was giving up socialising until we had the deposit we needed. It felt to me like it was an impossibility not to hit the Opera Bar at 5 p.m. on a Friday! How did people manage to go home instead? A radical change was needed, so we decided to commit to running the Sydney marathon, and to hit the gym for a couple of hours on Friday evenings until the urge to go out drinking had passed.

There's a thing called the 'goal gradient effect', which holds that as you start to see results and begin moving towards your target, you gain enthusiasm. In other words, the closer you get to a goal, the harder you try! That was certainly our experience. For the first few weeks, our new lifestyle felt unsustainable, but quite quickly we began ticking off milestones towards our goal. Just one year later, not only had we trudged our way through the Sydney marathon on a painfully hot day, but we'd also managed to pull together the deposit to buy the unit we wanted at Darling Harbour.

This is just our experience, and the journey is necessarily different for each person. Is it easier for couples with two incomes?

Yes, for sure. But it's not impossible on one income, even if does take longer to reach the goal. The key is to identify the big-ticket expenditure items, make a plan to save consistently, and then do whatever it takes to make sure you hit your target, even if it means selling a few consumer goods, working weekends, doing some overtime, getting a second job, or asking parents for a helping hand. *Whatever it takes!*

Buying your first property

So, let's say you've been working hard to save that first pool of money to invest, and you've finally reached the tipping point: you have enough to buy your first property! You've run the numbers and you're confident you can afford a quality investment and comfortably make the repayments now and into the future. How do you Buy Right?

Whether you end up purchasing at auction or private sale, the basic process itself is the same:

1. Preapproval
2. Planning the purchase
3. Searching
4. Due diligence (checking red flags and encumbrances, conducting building and pest inspections, and working out the right price to pay)
5. Legal review
6. Discussing terms with the agent so you know the vendor's preferred settlement and deposit terms
7. Understanding how the negotiation or auction will run and what the agent's rules are for the process
8. Negotiation
9. Exchange of contracts
10. Finance approval
11. Settlement.

Preapproval is step 1: get this in place before you think about anything else. We highly recommend seeking help with your finance from an investment-oriented mortgage broker. OK, we're probably biased – but it's worthwhile. Not only can a great mortgage broker find the right loan for you, he or she can advise you about structuring your loan in a way that will make it easier to purchase additional properties down the track. He or she can also advise on loan structuring for potential tax deductions and other tax-related benefits. This can save you a lot of money and headaches!

We go into detail about financing in chapter 10, and negotiation in chapter 8, so let's put those aside for now and dive into steps 2 and 3: planning and searching for a property.

About rent-vesting

When you apply for preapproval, you'll need to decide whether the property will be a home you'll live in for now as a stepping-stone property (which you may later retain as an investment property) or whether you intend to rent-vest. Rent-vesting is simply renting one property while being the landlord of another.

It isn't for everybody, but it can work well for those suited to it. You may not be able to afford a property you'd like to live in, for example, or you may not be mentally or emotionally ready for the responsibility of home ownership.

Before 2015, many young first-time property buyers adopted rent-vesting to take advantage of low interest rates and build a property portfolio. As interest rates have increased and borrowing has become harder, it's not as easy as it once was to use this strategy to buy multiple properties very quickly. The focus for property investors should now be on quality rather than quantity.

Some younger Aussies are choosing to live with their parents for longer to help them save for a deposit and get onto the housing ladder. Many parents are also choosing to help their kids by passing on some of their inheritance early, colloquially known as 'the bank of Mum and Dad'. The government is well aware that home ownership is a hot political issue, and as such regularly makes initiatives and schemes available at the federal level (such as first-homebuyer schemes) and the state level (such as stamp duty exemptions) to help first homebuyers. The grants and schemes available are ever-changing, so we can't summarise them easily here as the information will quickly become dated. A well-qualified mortgage broker, financial planner or buyer's agent should be able to steer you in the right direction to help keep you abreast of what's available.

 ## On planning

This may surprise you, but most buyers don't have a firm plan. Many have a vague plan – perhaps merely identifying a broad area where they'd like to live or invest, or a type of dwelling they're after. Many have no plan at all!

Without a plan, buying a property can be a stressful exercise. We've found that prospective buyers can:

- have unrealistic expectations of what their budget can afford them, leading to a sense of 'What I want doesn't exist'
- be misaligned with a partner (or other stakeholders in the decision-making process)
- have a limited understanding of market values, so they miss out at every turn to stronger buyers or bidders
- have too many options to choose from due to overly broad search criteria
- be unable to decide quickly enough to secure a suitable property
- experience a lack of support from agents, due to a lack of certainty on the agents' part that they're serious

- be disadvantaged by agents whom they've managed to get offside
- fear buying a lemon and procrastinate or get tied up in 'analysis paralysis'
- be uncertain about whether a target property is 'the one' (or even whether it's purchase-worthy).

There *is* a formula to finding the right property, though, and it's been tried and tested by hundreds of our clients. All it takes is some pragmatic thinking, having an honest conversation with yourself, and accepting that there's no such thing as a perfect property.

Properties are like people: no two are the same, and personalities and needs can change. There is such a thing as a 'high-scoring property', however: a property that's suitable for you now and into the future, and easily saleable if the time comes to sell.

Defining what a high-scoring property is for you gives you a handy roadmap that will stand you in good stead when your heart argues with your head. Specifying your criteria, knowing the geographic boundaries of the search, and adhering to your budget will equip you to hit open-for-inspections like a professional buyer.

How do you choose a property? This is how we do it in my business.

First of all: **budget** is fixed. We don't argue with the budget. Once you've sought appropriate lending advice and determined your desired budget and a firm upper price limit, we take note of it and start to set the other criteria.

Next, determine the **location**. What you're looking for will be affected by whether you're an owner occupier or an investor.

If you're an owner occupier, here are some questions to ask yourself:

- Where do you want to live?
- What does your current lifestyle look like?
- Where is your work located? How do you get there?
- Where is future work likely to be located?

- Do you enjoy going out? What neighbourhoods do you frequent?
- Where is family situated?
- Do schools or universities need to be factored in?

Some people have a firm idea of exactly where they wish to live, while others are open to a broad array of options. It doesn't matter if you're more open-minded about locations, or even if you're unfamiliar with what the city or region has to offer – you'll just have some extra homework and fun day trips ahead.

If you're an investor, you might like to ask yourself these questions:

- How much do you wish to spend on the acquisition? This will determine some of the areas you consider.
- How much rent do you need? This will determine the type of dwelling you target and, hence, some specific locations.
- Do you wish to diversify away from where you live (or where other investments are)?
- What types of tenants do you prefer? Professionals? Families? Singles? Students?
- Do you have personal future use in mind?

Next, consider **land size**, orientation, and street quality. How much space do you need (internally and externally)? Conversations with our clients often cover backyard size, future subdivision potential, garden arrangements, outdoor entertaining courtyards, and space for swimming pools.

Land value also plays a huge role in the discussion, which we discuss a little later. Consider, however, whether a quest for more land in your desired loactions may involve purchasing a compromised property – on a busier road, for example, or with railway noise, under a flight path, or with an odd-shaped block or south-facing living areas.

Next, we discuss the **condition** of the property, our client's ability to make improvements and fix things, and the funds they have on hand to pay for it. We canvass future works (such as renovations, extensions, or rebuilds) and their potential timing.

If you're putting all your capital into the purchase (which is typical of first homebuyers, whose borrowing capacity is a direct result of the strength of their deposit), you generally won't be able to fund immediate improvements, unless you're being gifted the money to do so.

Ask yourself about your financial capacity, your ability to renovate, and your appetite for a less-than-polished property. There's little fun in doing a hands-on renovation while you have a newborn, nor is there much reward in tackling re-stumping if you have limited resources to attend to all the things that may shake, crack, or break during the process. Being honest about your capacity to deal with properties in poorer condition is vital.

Finally, we challenge clients to separate their criteria into **'must-haves'** and **'nice-to-haves'**. You can list any number of attributes, from style and size to specific needs (such as natural light, a garage or sheds). This is typically the bulk of our initial planning conversations, and clients' criteria can spread over multiple pages. These are further refined over time, especially after viability back-testing.

My best purchasing advice is to select a property based on the must-have and nice-to-have list, and to stick to the must-haves. Put suitable agreements in place if you're co-purchasing – these might include tenants-in-common agreements, prenups and agreed exit clauses. Make a firm plan, with realistic and feasible criteria, to purchase a property that you can hold for the long term.

Does what you want exist? Viability back-testing

Cate has a science background, and she'll tell you that back-testing is an important part of many projects. Make sure that the needs and wants you've identified are achievable. Are there suitable properties in the geographic locations you have selected, and if so, are there enough of them for you to buy in a reasonable amount of time? How frequently do these properties come up?

A property search that yields fewer than six ideal properties in a year for a given area is going to be a tough project. You have no control over whether the type of property you want will be listed for sale. Sometimes the market could be flooded with five in a month, and then you could wait another ten months before the sixth eligible listing comes up. In a seller's market, you should anticipate competition, too: you can't assume you'll have a free run at the first eligible property that appeals to you.

Cate Bakos Property had a long assignment back in 2014 when a lovely family asked the team to find them a four-bedroom home in Yarraville's village. They had specific criteria, and it became obvious that their dream home was a four-in-one-year type of search. The team missed two, but secured their home with some off-market success almost a year into the assignment.

The next question may seem obvious, but many buyers go on for months deluding themselves and getting despondent: If what you want exists, does it exist on your budget?

'Champagne taste on a beer budget' is a common saying in the real estate industry. Cate's business occasionally gets clients who seem to hope that the team are genies in a bottle who can secure their dream property at a 30 per cent discount. If she senses that they're unfamiliar with pricing in their market (or have unreasonable expectations), she asks them to send links to five recently sold properties from the 'Sold' tab of a search engine. She stipulates that the links must be representative of a property they'd have been prepared to consider purchasing, the sale price must be within their budget, and the sale dates cannot be more than six months old.

If you conduct such a search and find *zero* properties, you'll need to reconsider your must-haves and nice-to-haves and make some compromises.

Making compromises using the Magic Quadrant

We find that more than 90 per cent of homebuyers get stuck at the onset of their property search, because they realise that what they're looking for is hard to find. They may feel that everything they like and that meets their criteria in their desired locations is outside of their budget.

The four key jigsaw pieces that need to fit together are not fitting. We call this puzzle the 'Magic Quadrant' (see figure 7.2). To every client who's stuck with their brief, we say, 'Just change ONE of the jigsaw pieces. Tell us which one you're prepared to be flexible on'. Every buyer has their own set of priorities – what one person may be prepared to sacrifice, another will not. Only one piece needs to change for the puzzle to fit together nicely.

Figure 7.2: the magic quadrant

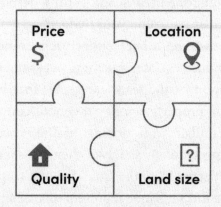

First is price. In most cases, price is the element we can't really adjust. Neither do we try to adjust our client's budget – their maximum purchase price. As mentioned earlier, as advisors, we work within the parameters we have, and price is often non-negotiable. For those who can change their price, however, a new, higher price limit may mean improved options.

Second is location. This is the jigsaw piece which more people are prepared to change. Cate once had buyers, for example, who were mad-keen on buying in the Melbourne suburb of Blackburn, yet every three-bedroom property which suited them was above their budget. She suggested they move their search band just a few kilometres east and explore Vermont as an option. They were delighted to find an established suburb which offered similar properties and matched their budget.

This often small change to a wish list can make a significant difference and, in nearly all cases, enables buyers to find the size, style, floor plan, and quality of property they're after at a lower price tag compared to the suburbs in which they were initially searching.

Third is land size. In all good, established suburbs in Australia's metro areas, the land component is usually the more significant item of value when we separate the house from the land. When you're prepared to sacrifice some of the land, therefore, you can buy in areas where ordinarily your budget wouldn't stretch, just by settling for a home on a half-block as opposed to a full block. This option isn't viable for everyone – investors, for example, should pay consideration to land-to-asset ratios – but it certainly is for some folks, such as downsizers who don't want the pressure of a large garden, or professionals who don't have the time (or need) for land. It is a great option for anyone who has 'good land size' at the bottom of their wish list.

The quality of the home is the final piece of the jigsaw puzzle. Again, compromising on this isn't for everyone. For many buyers, the mere thought of having to live through a renovation – or worse still, do the renovation themselves – is a nightmare. However, for buyers who are handy or have a partner who is trade-skilled, it can open up all kinds of opportunities. Not only that, adding value through clever improvements or renovations can have a positive effect in the longer term.

Two case studies

Every single property journey is different. Every single client I've worked with has had to formulate an initial plan with me. A road map. A strategy. A blueprint. Only once we document a plan can we start shopping.

Some plans are more difficult to construct than others, because we often find that new clients can have unrealistic expectations, have had their fingers burnt with purchase attempts, are not on the same page as their partner, or have a complexity to their brief which means it will be challenging.

I recall a tough brief many years ago with a lovely Yarraville couple. They had firm criteria and a list of eligible streets. They'd been searching for months when they sought my help, and there was no mystery about why once I profiled and overlaid all their requirements: it became evident that they only had a choice of some six or seven houses in the entire array of streets they'd selected. They wanted to be within the Yarraville village, needed a three-bedroom house, wanted not only off-street parking but a garage or roller door to hide a marked police car from visibility, and they specifically wanted a single-fronted Victorian house.

This was no mean feat. If the average homeowner sells every seven to ten years, we were facing a wait of at least 15 months by the law of averages before the next property came up... and the market was moving fast.

I sat down with them for an hour to prioritise their wish list and determine which elements they could budge on. They decided that the three bedrooms could actually be two, and the Victorian house could be *any* period house, but the hidden car option was not open to change. The search recommenced with these new must-haves, and within a fortnight, a local agent had found us a double-storey, two bedroom-plus-study single-fronted Victorian cottage with a side driveway and roller-door carport – within budget.

A more recent client's journey had equally important but very different criteria. His wish to have the firm option of a flatmate in his villa unit meant that the two bedrooms both had to be of a decent size, and preferably not sharing a wall. Having a toilet separate from the bathroom and the option of having a hand-wash station in a separate laundry was important too.

He presented an off-market opportunity he'd received from an agent to my attention. The property was a villa, and the block was a boutique cluster of three in an attractive street in one of his desired postcodes. The problem was the second bedroom: it measured a mere 2.7 metres wide. This would make it difficult for a tenant to fit in a queen-sized bed and two side tables, and would thus make it an undesirable rental. I ruled it out and advised him to keep looking.

Buyers who bend on their must-have criteria make a serious mistake. If the element they flagged as integral isn't a feature in their new property, they'll likely experience regret or frustration once they settle the purchase.

Sorting out the must-haves from the nice-to-haves should be done before going shopping. Always. You're not buying a dress or a pair of sunglasses – you're buying a property.

Applying the land-to-asset ratio

We discussed the importance of land-to-asset ratio in chapter 6. It's not an often-used metric in our industry, but it should be. A Melbourne-based property planner named David Johnston registered the term early in the last decade, and it's a powerful tool for measuring the health of a property's prospects.

To recap, land-to-asset ratio is the ratio of a property's land content to the total asset value – to the value of the land when benchmarked against the value of any dwelling plus improvements on this land. The basic principle is that over time, land appreciates (rises in value), while dwellings depreciate (lose value).

We looked at how land-to-asset ratio affects apartments and new properties in chapter 6; now, let's unpack how it relates to established houses.

Here's an example in Melbourne's bayside suburb of Carrum: a house on nearly 1000 square metres of land just minutes from the beach, which sold for $1 million in July 2018. It's likely that the buyer who purchased this property did so because of its development potential – the subdivided allotment directly next to it (comprising three dwellings) demonstrates what it could possibly become.

Let's assume the old house on it has depreciated over the years to a current value of $50,000. That would make the land-to-asset ratio a massive 95 per cent – the land component represents the vast majority of the value.

As we stated, land appreciates and dwellings depreciate, so it's fair to say that the capital growth prospects of this property are very strong. The diminishing value of the dwelling is tiny, because it was only worth $50,000 at the time of purchase. The land portion, however, represents $950,000. At a conservative estimate of 5 per cent per annum capital growth, the land would gain $47,500 in value in the first year. This rate of growth far surpasses the rate of depreciation of the dwelling.

Compare that to a brand-new townhouse on a block of three, also in Carrum. A gorgeous three-bedroom property, it sold in March 2019 for $725,000. We know from the other Carrum property that the land would have been worth around $950,000 before the block was subdivided, so we can calculate broadly that the land value of this particular property is approximately $225,000. That makes the land-to-asset ratio 23.7 per cent.

As a result, the rate of dwelling depreciation will eclipse the rate of land appreciation, just as it did in the examples we discussed in chapter 6. And that means the buyer is likely to see their property value diminish in the first few years of ownership. As we said earlier, it's like driving a brand-new car off the lot – it depreciates immediately and is coming off its highest base when brand new.

So, what are the limitations of using the land-to-asset ratio? There are two major points to note:

1. It isn't an exact science, only an approximation. Analysing the precise dollar value of a block per square metre is impossible. Variables such as orientation, slope, 'highest and best use', zoning, overlays, easements, neighbours, noise, street quality, market timing, competing buyers on the day, and so on all have an impact. The land sale of one site can't determine another site's value; it can only indicate what another developer will likely pay in the same market.

2. Aiming for a higher land-to-asset ratio in the quest for maximised capital growth comes with two downsides. First, the dwelling will be particularly rugged if the ratio is high. If you intend to rent the property, this will precipitate tenant grumbles, requests for improvement, lower rental prospects, and possibly a less desirable tenant. Second, the cashflow equation will be harder on you as an investor, since you'll have lower rent and higher maintenance expenses as well as having to pay a higher price to secure that generous allotment of land.

David Johnston cites an 'ideal' land-to-asset ratio of around 70 per cent. I'm not so prescriptive and I can forgive an asset with a ratio closer to 85 per cent, depending on the investor's willingness to manage the tenant's rights and expectations. What we aim to avoid, as I stated earlier, is a land-to-asset ratio of 50 per cent or less.

Familiarising yourself with locales

Many buyers will be very familiar with their chosen purchase area. But if you're opting to search beyond your familiar suburbs, it's advantageous to become aware of the different pockets, streets, and points of interest.

A few reconnaissance missions over weekends will give you a firm feel for an area, and in particular stronger confidence about the pros and cons of each pocket, and the property value differential between pockets. You should look to answer the following questions:

- Where are the important things for you, or for your ideal tenant, such as the train station, bus stops, local shops, work and businesses, schools, cafés, medical facilities, parks, sports clubs, and theatres?
- Where are the expensive pockets?
- Where are the 'dodgy' pockets – the areas with higher crime or more noise, that are less aesthetically pleasing, inconvenient, or dislocated, or that have mixed zoning?
- Where are your favoured pockets based on the criteria and your lifestyle, or the lifestyle of your target tenant?

Go to auctions and open-for-inspections

Check out some open-for-inspections and sales in the area to get a feel for your competitors, the agents, and the way things roll.

Just bear in mind that to get the best out of local real estate agents, it's important to be clear about your intent. Agents won't appreciate feigned enthusiasm if you aren't yet in the market. Let them know that you're planning to buy imminently, but be honest with them about the current inspection being a familiarisation exercise only. Don't give them purchaser-signals and be careful not to abuse their time and energy. Purchaser-signals include:

- asking for contracts of sale or section 32s (called 'disclosure statements' in some states)

- pummelling them with questions about the vendor's desired terms, settlement periods, reasons for sale, and so on
- asking about bidding activity at auction.

Save up your local agent's help and favours for when you're a dedicated buyer. However, if you have general questions about real estate rules, suburb character, differentiation between suburb pockets, or even comparable sale properties, you'll find that most friendly agents are happy to chat quite openly with you at a property inspection, provided that there aren't a high volume of buyers attending.

Like all humans, agents generally enjoy respect and banter. They're regularly greeted with scepticism and disdain, so a memorable buyer will likely earn some favours. As they say, 'It's easier to attract bees with honey'.

Observing some auctions will also be highly beneficial. It's interesting to observe how an auctioneer's antics entertain a crowd and how their tactics control bidding. Take note of:

- how long their preamble goes for, the declaration of the auction rules, and how they describe the various properties
- how they usually extract initial bids from the crowd
- buyer behaviour and visible nerves
- the half-time break, and those auctions which don't require a half-time break
- vendor bids
- bidding increments and when they start to diminish
- the auctioneer's notification to the crowd when the property reaches the reserve price, and the change of pace of bidding after this point
- the auctioneer's efforts to continue extracting bids from buyers
- the final 'auction call' – 'Going once, going twice, for the *thirrrrrrrd* and FINAL call…'

Auctioneer styles vary; you'll get good insights into what you can expect by seeing the local auctioneers at work. You may also get some good insights into what not to do by observing other buyers' bungles! We talk more about bidding and negotiation tactics in the next chapter.

 ## Case study of a great start

Back in 2011, I participated in a first-homebuyer event alongside a lovely industry buddy, a mortgage broker called Steve. We teamed up and ran a series of small seminars over a few weeknights for buyers who were keen to explore the idea of property investing or home-buying.

The nights weren't always well-attended, but we enjoyed the questions and the interactions with our participants. For many, it was early days on their journey and the evenings focused on the initial planning phase – usually addressing minimum deposit savings and all of the fiscal elements a young buyer would need to consider in order to be purchase-ready. Steve chatted about the finance and I addressed the property side of the equation. At one of these sessions, I met a young prospective investor I'll call 'Anna'.

Some months later, Anna contacted us. She was in her twenties and was serious about buying a property. She was well aware of her budget and borrowing capacity constraints and had decided that she'd be prepared to rent-vest initially – buying an investment property and renting her own home. Her ultimate goal was to build up to buying her own home in suburban Melbourne one day, preferably on the beach. A big goal? For sure, but a very realistic one if she could stick to the plan.

Although Anna had been saving aggressively, her funds on hand were limited. After some discussion, she decided to make a purchase and pay lenders mortgage insurance instead of spending more time saving to achieve a 20 per cent deposit. Steve arranged the preapproval, and we started working together to find Anna a great capital-growth performer that could generate her enough equity to springboard into another investment property.

Her first purchase was in Deer Park, and it's fair to say that back in June 2012, Deer Park was not yet a gentrified suburb. In fact, houses in Deer Park were affordable by Melbourne measures and situated just 17 kilometres west of the city. My analysis had led me to a handful of established areas in the suburb, serviced by rail, that had promising capital-growth potential based on the expansion of the urban growth boundary and the proliferation of a lot of land releases considerably further out than these older, established neighbourhoods.

Anna bought a house for $276,400 on a 625 square metre block in one of these areas, near a shopping centre and primary schools. She rented it back to the previous owners at a 5 per cent gross rental return for a while, until they ultimately moved on to buy another home of their own. Anna's rent peaked at $340 per week.

Her Deer Park property performed for her as planned, so in late 2017, Anna and I targeted Ballarat for investment property number two. We selected Ballarat because Anna was targeting a neutral cashflow scenario, much like that of Deer Park – meaning that she wanted the income from the property to cover the costs and break roughly even. She wanted to be able to comfortably afford her own rent and living expenses, maintenance on her properties – and to be able to continue saving too. We also decided to target a block of land with developer potential. Not that Anna had development plans, but she did plan to sell and crystallise a gain when it was time to buy her own home, so we wanted to capture some developer appeal to bolster her chances of a tidy profit.

We planned our voyage to this exciting regional city and shortlisted over ten suitable contenders to inspect. A neatly renovated cottage in Ballarat East (see figure 7.3) scored highly, and within 48 hours Anna had an executed contract of sale for $330,000.

The property leased immediately for $330 per week, delivering a neat 5.2 per cent gross rental return almost seamlessly.

Combined with the depreciation benefits, Anna found herself in positive cashflow territory very quickly and recognised that unlike Deer Park, this property was a long-term keeper.

Her next property, she reminded me, would be her home.

When she got in touch again, a bank valuation on her Ballarat property proved rewarding! Over less than a four-year period, the cottage had delivered a whopping 11 per cent per annum capital-growth return. So, we jumped into gear with her owner-occupier property strategy: Anna sold Deer Park for $540,000 and had a nest egg, access to equity and a spring in her step.

Figure 7.3: Anna's Ballarat East investment

Anna's home wish list was realistic and exciting. She wanted to live by the beach, have rail and local shopping nearby, and particularly, really wanted a yard for her dog. The puppy was on order for a March arrival, which did make me smile. No pressure, of course!

We worked on a search band from Elwood through to the Mordialloc Creek, shortlisting every available dwelling within her budget that offered a yard. Anna inspected diligently every Saturday, and when I received an excited 'Green light! Green light!' email, I had a good feeling about the villa in question.

The inspection didn't disappoint. There were only five units in the block, and it was situated a very short walk from beach, shops, and station. With recent roof works completed, and offering a generous yard and decked area, a superbly renovated interior, security-gate access, and solar panels, I knew it was worth pursuing.

Of course, others felt the same way, and the agents fielded offers from four competing buyers for this gorgeous villa. Happily for Anna though, we were successful, and she's now enjoying her new home and new puppy.

Being a contrarian – Cate's experience

Being a contrarian sounds so exciting when you read about contrarian investors who made serious money when everyone else was sitting cautiously on their hands. Nevertheless, when the opportunity arises, it's surprising how many people who say they wish they'd taken the chance last time still don't do it *this* time. Staying safe and comfortable is our default human response.

I knew from my time as a selling agent that the ebbs and flows of real estate markets could flummox buyers, so when the global financial crisis struck, I quickly identified it as a big opportunity. While the crisis felt quite frightening, I was aware that my husband and I had reasonable job security and an ability to pay down debt. We had chosen to rent-vest, biding our time to strike when an exciting opportunity arose.

All we needed was our landlord hiking up our rent to initiate the move. I'd spotted an opportunity on Gumtree.com.au and we inspected a rundown little maisonette cottage within three houseblocks of the sand on Aspendale beach. We secured this rugged little gem (which I discussed in chapter 5) for $310,000 in December 2008, when the headlines were all doom and gloom. Our family members thought we were insane for buying during such a risky period, but we knew that $310,000 for a house in this pocket was a potentially lucrative buy. Interestingly, the pigeon-pair house next door sold for $420,000 two and a half years later: a 35 per cent increase in value.

We prepped our preapprovals and didn't stop there, purchasing several more properties. Lending was easier because the Reserve Bank of Australia had eased rates, and the new federal Labor Government had introduced all kinds of incentives to stimulate the economy (which was in what felt like financial freefall). Australia dodged all kinds of bullets for varying reasons, but our willingness to pursue investment acquisitions in a cautious market rewarded us. We look back on our contrarian stance and feel proud that we backed ourselves when so many ridiculed us.

Since the global financial crisis, Australia has experienced its fair share of contrarian opportunities. I've enjoyed assisting clients with their respective journeys through various downturns that have impacted our property markets. The thing about being a buyer's agent is that when you're working at the coalface, sentiment and trends are palpable. We get incredible insights into market turns that many economists and analysts sometimes sneer at, until they see the data translate.

I recall Pete telling me in 2020, when COVID-19 gripped our shores, that he'd posted one of my articles on Twitter and noted a fair amount of ridicule of my optimism about the market turn. As it turned out, I was right. Thank goodness I didn't watch the Twitter feed!

Figure 7.4 represents my clients' acquisitions in March and April 2020 during the onset of COVID-19 in Melbourne.

The most mind-boggling aspect to this, which isn't shown on the chart, is that we sustained horrible price falls over a three-week period before the market stabilised and took off again. This represented the shortest and sharpest downturn in Melbourne's property history, ever. The clients who took action in 2020 look back and marvel; those who froze fearfully and chose to wait it out are full of regret.

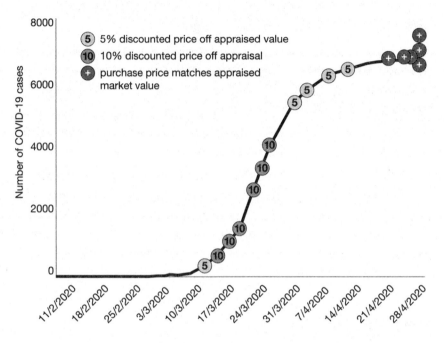

Figure 7.4: client acquisitions in March/April 2020 and number of COVID-19 cases in Melbourne

SOURCE: DEPARTMENT OF HEALTH, STATES & TERRITORIES REPORT 2/5/2020

 Being a contrarian – Pete's experience

When I decided to pull the plug on my professional career as an accountant, it was interesting to note how negative much of the feedback was. I was a lot younger back then, and when I wrote my first book and started doing TV breakfast shows on Channel 7 and Channel 10, I worried a lot more about what people might say.

The interesting thing is that what I feared most – that some people would criticise or mock me – actually happened! But so what? A mentor of mine explained to me that the first time this sort of thing happens, it's painful. We're hardwired to take criticism to heart and notice negative feedback more than we notice the positive stuff. The good news is that the second time it happens it's a bit less painful, and then the third time a bit less painful again... until, eventually, it all just bounces off. A bit like anything else, the more you do it, the easier it gets.

If you decide to build a property portfolio, it's quite likely people will question whether that's a good idea. Sometimes this is well meant, because friends and family don't want to see you make a mistake. Sometimes people simply don't like you taking a different path from the norm, because it's challenging to them, and often it holds up a mirror to their own journey and decisions.

As Cate has noted, it's hard to go against the grain as an investor. The longer I work in the housing market as a property professional, the more I realise that the cycles will never change, driven as they are by fear and greed: fear of losing money on the way down, and greed at wanting to gain in the boom times. Getting a handle on purchasing psychology truly is key to being a contrarian.

Purchasing psychology

Human psychology can really rain on a property buyer's parade; psychologically induced worries can strike when we're least expecting it. Pete prepares his buyers for 'post-purchase dissonance', a common feeling of panic or regret shortly after a purchase, but many types of decision-making doubts can grip us.

You're probably familiar with *FOMO – the fear of missing out*. This usually strikes in a hot market when prices are soaring and supply feels tight. We've also coined the term *'FOBBABO' – fear of buying before a better option* comes up. This can strike any time, but it's more prevalent in a market where prices are falling or static. Buyers are often concerned that they'll commit to purchasing a suitable property, only to find that a better or cheaper purchase opportunity comes along. We've seen many a good acquisition opportunity thwarted by this one.

Here are some of the less discussed psychological blockers:

- **The fear of pushing a partner into a property that they're not enthusiastic about.** Often in partnerships, one person takes more of a lead in the property quest than the other. This doesn't necessarily mean that the other person is not keen on the property or purchasing strategy; it may just mean that they're shyer or less energetic. But when partners aren't quite on the same page, trouble can strike if the less-inclined partner gives the impression that they're agreeing to purchase out of sheer fatigue. This pressure on the dominant decision-maker can lead them to second-guess their selection.

- **The fear of dishonouring a late loved one when spending an inheritance.** Sadly, this fear often strikes buyers who've received a special inheritance. The buyer's determination to honour the memory of the loved one who gifted them the money can quickly contradict the intent of the gesture. Their quest for a great property that makes them happy morphs into an obsession with finding the perfect property – but there's no such thing as perfection in property.

- **Listening to others** is a constant issue, particularly for first homebuyers: when parents or friends weigh in, the purchase strategy can quickly become blurred. Once confusion sets in and the buyer starts scrambling to please everyone, their once-achievable brief becomes a messy assortment of unattainable criteria. They may make random suggestions to their buyer's agent that are misaligned with their original must-haves, and become frustrated and often fatigued or despairing.

- **Trying to save a few dollars** can set a buyer back significantly when the resulting smaller budget isn't commensurate with their expectations. We see this a lot, particularly when interest rates are rising; buyers can then spend months searching hopelessly in a rising market. We helped several buyers during 2020 and 2021 who had shaved their budget to try to reduce their debt, only to find that as the market rose, they were forced to increase their budget again, and ultimately spent more than they would have if they'd just stuck with their original budget and purchased sooner. If you've set your budget at a level where you know you'll comfortably be able to afford the repayments, don't second-guess it.

- **The fear of not deserving a great property** is last in this list, but not least. Humility is a laudable character trait, but when a buyer talks themselves out of an aspirational property merely because they don't feel worthy of it, regret can strike. We always stress the importance of future-proofing a purchase – making sure that the property will meet their foreseeable needs over the next five years – but we remind our clients that in the worst case, if they end up being really unhappy with the property, they can sell.

Get your mindset right, stick to your plan and your must-have criteria, and you'll give yourself the best chance of making a great investment in both good times and challenging times. Of course, it's also vital to do your diligence on each potential property purchase!

Doing due diligence

Cate remembers years ago hearing a conveyancer say, 'I had to be firm. I told the caller that their lack of planning was *not* going to be my emergency'.

What was she talking about?

She had had a prospective client purchase at auction without a contract review, and it wasn't until the contract landed on her desk that she could shed light on the issues that this buyer was going to face. We're not sure what the specific issues were – the title could have been quirky (such as a company title or stratum title), or the owners corporation outgoings could have been extortionate – but her point was clear. The purchaser hadn't allowed her to do any due diligence prior to auction, and now his or her woes were threatening to plague the conveyancer's morning.

We work with purchasers and agents every single day, and face plenty of situations in which lack of planning can create stress and unnecessary issues for all concerned. Some can result in dire outcomes; others can merely be a cause of irritation.

Due diligence is particularly time-sensitive before auctions. Cate's business has an internal policy that requires clients to confirm all auctions that they want the business to assist with by midday on Wednesday. Cate and her team can't thoroughly conduct due diligence if the request comes in on the Thursday or the Friday, as they have a host of things to coordinate, so they now politely decline the job if it rolls in after lunchtime on Wednesday.

The due diligence you should be doing before a property purchase (or having your buyer's agent do) includes the following:

- **A physical inspection.** This is easily arranged, but if the property is tenanted or if the vendor is strict about open times, you may not be able to facilitate an inspection at the last minute before an auction, for example.

- **A building and pest inspection.** This is risky to try to arrange at late notice, because not only may you be unable to get access to the property, the builder may not be available.

- **A thorough contract review.** Some solicitors and conveyancers may be able to manage a same-day review, but even following the review, it can take time to renegotiate special conditions, order certificates, explore missing certificates and declarations, talk to building surveyors, follow up with the council, and other related tasks. You may then also need time to negotiate variations to the contract. A variety of other points may also need to be investigated, depending on the property. This could involve, for example, conversing with the owners corporation manager, talking to property managers, and checking easements. The consumer checklist here could be a good guide: consumer.vic.gov.au/housing/buying-and-selling-property/checklists/due-diligence.

- **Arranging your deposit and payment method.** You should already have preapproval (right?!) – that's step 1, remember? If you start your property search without finance approval in place, deposit funds on hand, and a clear understanding of timeframes required for settlement, you're potentially setting yourself up for an emergency. However, some buyers keep their deposit funds in bank accounts that aren't easily accessible (such as term deposits, international accounts, or accounts that require bank assistance to move or transfer money). Some buyers assume that they don't have a maximum daily transfer limit from the account that their deposit funds are in.

The number of times we've struck panic at auction when the agreed amount of deposit funds can't be paid is amazing. Cate carries a blank cheque around for this reason! It's her emergency 'not linked to an account but affords the buyer an extra day to sort their deposit out' cheque, and it's there in her wallet specifically for those times when post-auction payment attempts strike a glitch.

About contract reviews

'No contract review, no purchase!' is one of Cate's favourite sayings. There are many issues that she, as a buyer's agent, can spot in a contract, but a qualified legal professional will often identify many more potential problems. Neglecting to get a quality contract review can be expensive in the long run.

There are myriad potential issues that qualified legal representatives can identify.

A review will reveal red flags such as strata issues, compulsory acquisition overlays, and restrictive covenants. Permits, certificates, owner-builder documentation, and warranty insurance are also frequently raised. A thorough conveyancer or solicitor will check the online photographs and floor plan of the property in question, and often they'll request more paperwork from the vendor. Depending on the age of the works, the council planning requirements, and the extent of the work carried out, there may be missing documentation.

Paperwork deficiency strikes more regularly than you might imagine. Cate finds herself requesting extra documentation for permitted works on a weekly basis. It's when the works should have come with a permit but don't that there is an issue. Once a property settles, the purchaser inherits the liability for any non-permitted works, so understanding the risk, the potential cost, the potential stress, and the impact on future insurance claims is critical.

Provide photos or observations to your legal representative if you sense that any works have recently been carried out on a property you're shortlisting, especially if the online photographs don't show these works.

Information about neighbouring properties that have advertised planning applications for extensions, renovations, or developments must also be included in a contract of sale, and a thorough contract review will shed light on any upcoming changes you should know about.

Another upset relates to special conditions being added to the contract by the vendor's solicitor, or the purchaser's statutory rights being deleted. Following is an example of the General Conditions in a standard Victorian Contract of Sale; removing any of these can result in removing some legal rights. Resolving any pre-settlement issues in this regard can be stressful at times.

Special condition 14 – Settlement

Settlement must be conducted between the hours of 10.00 a.m. and 4.00 p.m. unless the parties agree otherwise. If settlement is not conducted by 4.00 p.m. then settlement is deferred until the next business day. In the event of a deferral of the settlement date pursuant to the provisions of this Special Condition the Purchaser shall be deemed to have breached this Contract and must pay penalty interest together with a settlement rebooking fee of $330.00.

Special condition 15 – Default

15.1 If the Vendor gives to the Purchaser notice of default under this contract the default will not be remedied until the Purchaser has:

(a) remedied the default or, if the default is incapable of remedy, paid compensation to the Vendor to the Vendor's satisfaction; and

(b) paid all costs and expenses incurred by the Vendor as a result of the default including without limitation legal costs (including disbursements) on a solicitor/client basis any additional costs incurred by the Vendor; including, without limitation, interest and borrowing expenses and payment of default interest.

15.2 The Purchaser agrees and acknowledges that if the Contract ends by a default notice given by the Vendor in accordance with General Condition 27, then:

(a) Any part of the Deposit that exceeds 10% of the Price (if any) ("The Part Of The Deposit That Exceeds 10%") is forfeited to the Vendor as the Vendor's absolute property, whether any part of The Part Of The Deposit That Exceeds 10% has been paid or not;

(b) The provisions of this special condition 15.2 and any other provision in this Contact is subject to the provisions of the *Sale of Land Act 1962* (Vic).

(c) The parties agree and acknowledge that, for the avoidance of doubt, nothing in this special condition 15.2 affects the operation of General Condition 28.4(a), and

(d) The parties agree and acknowledge that if special condition 15.2 is unenforceable for whatever reason, General Condition 28.4(d) shall apply in relation to The Part Of The Deposit That Exceeds 10% and any other part of the Price paid.

Special condition 16 – Default Expenses

16.1 If the Purchaser defaults in complying with any of its obligations as set out in this Contract, the Purchaser shall pay, in addition to any other moneys payable to the Vendor, any legal costs on a Solicitor own client basis incurred by the Vendor as a result of any such default by the Purchaser.

16.2 The Purchaser must pay to the Vendor all costs and expenses incurred by the Vendor due to any breach of this Contract by the Purchaser.

16.3 The Purchaser agrees that the reasonably foreseeable loss the Vendor may suffer due to the Purchaser's breach of this contract may include, without limitation, interest payable by the Vendor in relation to loans secured on the Land for the period from the date the Balance is payable under this Contract to the date the Balance is paid, interest incurred on any purchase by the Vendor which is incurred as a result of the Purchaser's default, interest on bridging finance obtained by the Vendor for the same period to cover the Vendor's intended use of the Price and the costs of that bridging finance and, if the Vendor is usually accommodated in the Land, accommodation costs incurred by the Vendor and the cost of storing the Vendor's property usually kept in the land.

Special Condition 17 – Settlement Re-Scheduling fee

The Purchaser agrees to pay the Vendor's Solicitor's costs of $330.00 (GST inclusive) to reschedule settlement should the Purchaser default and fail to settle on the agreed settlement date. The re-scheduling fee is to be paid to the Vendor's Solicitors at settlement.

Take, for example the 'loss or damage' condition shown on the next page. This clause provisions for up to $5000 to be withheld in trust while the vendor remedies damage; often, we find this condition has been removed by a special condition overriding it. While plenty of solicitors don't like their conditions being tampered with, a thorough legal review gives the purchaser a chance to negotiate them.

24. Loss or damage before settlement

24.1 The vendor carries the risk of loss or damage to the property until settlement.

24.2 The vendor must deliver the property to the purchaser at settlement in the same condition it was on the day of sale, except for fair wear and tear.

24.3 The purchaser must not delay settlement because one or more of the goods is not in the condition required by general condition 24.2 but may claim compensation from the vendor after settlement.

24.4 The purchaser may nominate an amount not exceeding $5,000 to be held by a stakeholder to be appointed by the parties if the property is not in the condition required by general condition 24.2 at settlement.

24.5 The nominated amount may be deducted from the amount due to the vendor at settlement and paid to the stakeholder, but only if the purchaser also pays an amount equal to the nominated amount to the stakeholder.

24.6 The stakeholder must pay the amounts referred to in general condition 24.5 in accordance with the determination of the dispute, including any order for payment of the costs of the resolution of the dispute.

By the time a final inspection rolls around, it may have been several months since contracts of sale were exchanged. Settlement is usually just days away, and sometimes there is insufficient time for a vendor to repair fresh damages. On occasion, too, difficult vendors may not be inclined to repair damage. It's then a challenge to have the vendor hand over the property in the same condition as it was on the date of sale, and you have no clause giving you a right to be compensated if they refuse to do so.

Discovering 'orders' on properties is another significant benefit of a contract review. Orders can range far and wide, and some that we've been privy to relate to serious issues such as combustible cladding on taller buildings. Often an order can spell trouble for a purchaser.

Contract reviews can also uncover special levies for expensive issues that may crop up in a strata development. We've seen plenty of horrible special levies for things like underpinning or asbestos removal. Sometimes a sign of issues can be multiple owners selling their units in the block at the same time. This can be a sad necessity for owners who don't have the cashflow or the fiscal appetite to pay the levy.

Zoning, planning restrictions, encumbrances, and caveats are always checked in a thorough contract review, too. It's important that your legal representatives know about any requirements you have, and any future plans for renovation or development of the property. For example, if you want a property to develop and the property you're investigating has a 'Single Dwelling Covenant', it won't be a viable purchase for you.

Know exactly what purchaser details should go on the contract of sale

If your company or trust (or other ownership entity) is going to be purchasing the property, rather than you individually, make sure you detail it correctly when signing the contract. Failing to do so can create more stress than you might imagine.

If you're co-purchasing, ensure the details of your co-purchaser and their percentage of ownership is documented thoroughly at the time of purchase. Making changes is quite difficult and can be expensive. In the case of an incorrect entity on the contract for a self-managed super fund purchase, the issues created can be highly costly.

Buyers with different name spellings on identification documentation (such as anglicised names on one document and original given names on passports, or maiden-name documentation that is yet to be formally updated) can face issues closer to settlement when bank staff pick up on the conflicting ID. If this happens within days (or hours) of settlement, it will likely impact your ability to settle on time, and you could face hefty delay penalties.

Satisfy any special conditions promptly

Another serious planning failure relates to settlement and special condition acceptance. If a contract has been subject to an approval of something, you need to heed the timeframe given and demonstrate that you've made every attempt to fulfil the condition.

Precedent cases do exist in which buyers have been forced to settle on a property despite not fulfilling their finance clause, merely because they couldn't demonstrate that they'd made a clear effort to obtain the finance by the due date. They left it to the last minute!

Assuming a vendor will agree to an extension request is risky. It's your responsibility, as the buyer, to monitor and manage critical dates – this isn't something that every conveyancer or solicitor will do. If a critical date passes without you confirming that you've satisfied a condition (for example, you're satisfied with the building and pest report findings, or finance approval has been granted), the contract will be deemed to be unconditional.

An unconditional contract means that the purchase is official, and deposit monies are not refundable. The most significant risks arise here when buyers purchase an asset that their lender does not support. Due diligence, legal reviews, and effective communication with banks and brokers are absolutely essential to mitigate this risk, and rushing a significant purchase or taking shortcuts is unthinkable!

We go into much more detail on financing and properties that lenders like or don't like in chapter 10. In the next chapter, we take a look at bidding and negotiation tactics.

Key points in this chapter

· Spend less than you earn!

· Getting started in property will require a strong saving habit (unless you have wealthy parents).

· Always carry out thorough due diligence on any property purchase.

8

Bidding and negotiation

Auctions are the dominant method of buying property in the inner and middle-ring suburbs of Melbourne and Sydney – but this can vary depending on market threats (such as a pandemic), the time of year, and the state of the market. Lending crackdowns by the Australian Prudential Regulation Authority (APRA); the Royal Commission into Misconduct in the Banking, Superannuation and Financial Services Industry; and COVID-19 lockdowns have all had an impact. In the wake of stricter lending conditions and rising interest rates, auction clearance rates lowered in the capital cities, and bidder numbers also reduced. However, we saw bidder and listing numbers increase in the post-COVID-19 recovery period.

Auction pass-ins (which occur when the top bid does not meet the reserve price) became a sign of the times during COVID-19 rather than a reflection of a compromised or low-scoring property. Many good properties passed in, and buyers relied more on 'subject to finance' clauses and private sale opportunities. Agents are more likely to recommend a private sale campaign when economic times are tougher.

Buyers, sellers, and agents had to adapt to doing significantly more negotiation during this time. Agents accepted that their auction process relied upon:

- remaining in close contact with prospective buyers throughout the campaign to gauge their intention (and ability) to bid
- preparing the vendor for a pass-in and subsequent negotiation
- allowing adequate time for this post-auction negotiation
- facilitating 'subject to finance' offers and the steps that follow (valuer access, follow-up with solicitors, communication with vendors and back-up buyers, and hosting open-for-inspections while the property is still under contract)
- being prepared to resell the property if the conditional sale does not proceed.

During tough times, agents are required to pivot from auction to private sale, and their buyer and vendor conversations involve caution around fear and disappointment.

During healthier market times, however, agents in these capital cities can enjoy the spoils that auctions provide. Well-attended auctions with spirited bidding often provide excellent results for vendors and their agents alike. Often a record price for a street or a suburb will occur through an auction. In addition to the kudos of a high sales result (and a rewarding commission payment), agents also benefit from the unconditional sale that an auction provides. Unlike a private sale with finance (or other) clauses and conditions, an auction result generally means that the property sale is unconditional, and no further buyer-related risk burdens the agent or their vendor.

Not all auction campaigns are devoid of private sale elements though. A buyer can place a pre-auction offer that leads to a negotiation. Alternatively, an auction property could fail to sell at auction, and this, too, will lead to a private sale negotiation. Both are detailed later in this chapter.

Bidding tactics

Auctions are usually dreaded, sometimes feared, and often avoided.

Auctions have been around since as early as 500 BC during the Roman Empire, and the word 'auction' in Latin means 'I increase'. While it's human behaviour to avoid price increases (whether through auctions or multiple-buyer private sales), competitive bidding is often key to attaining the prize. Avoiding it may mean avoiding the prize itself.

When a buyer has success at auction, can they ever put it down to bidding tactics? Absolutely! The number of people we've met who believe that auction success is solely based on budget is surprising. Plenty of buyers believe that bidding style has zero impact on their chances of success.

Of course, we know that some auction results are a perfect correlation with budget. A willing buyer who is prepared to fight in a price war will always have an increased chance of success.

In other auctions, luck can play a key role, and the outcome can surprise even the most seasoned of us. For example, a key buyer may drop out of the race at the last minute. A bidder may get stuck in traffic and miss the auction. A buyer could lose their job, rendering their finance preapproval invalid. Maybe a newly listed competing property could steal some hearts and reduce the buyer pool.

However, bidding tactics – carefully planned action to achieve a specific end – are a separate issue. The property community often debates whether tactics are advantageous or useless. Some argue that a tactical bidder has no greater or lesser impact than any other bidder, with the final result coming down to the winning bidder's budget.

We completely disagree.

They're assuming that every other potential bidder feels no fear, intimidation, awkwardness, or embarrassment. Yet there are humans out there who would rather miss out on a property than stand in a public space and shout out bids. Like the fear of public speaking – glossophobia – this is very common.

The impact of a confident, assertive bidder staring another bidder down cannot be underestimated. If the other bidder was already uncomfortable and now also feels intimidated, their chances of success diminish.

In our years in the field, we've seen countless examples of bidder behaviour in response to intimidatory or assertive bidding. Despite any amount of planning, people can find it difficult to think strategically under that kind of pressure. They could also struggle to communicate effectively with their partner with any budget reassessment discussions – and we all know how much of a pressure-cooker atmosphere an auctioneer can create during the final stages of an auction call while a hundred other people may be watching on.

Buyers have often come forward after the hammer has fallen to ask for our card, or to advise us that they thought we had a significantly stronger budget than we actually did. Agents have commented on our bidding style and have sometimes told us when one of their earmarked buyers decided under the pressure of the auction not to bid.

The most critical task a capable bidder faces is reducing the time for bidders to rethink their budget or determine an upper limit while the auctioneer is in full flight.

Signs of bidder nerves

Buyers are usually unaware, but any of the following hallmarks can enable an opposing bidder to read their nerves:

- Pacing
- Smoking
- Fiddling with their hands

- Continual checking of their watch before the auction bell rings
- Partners standing together as still as a pair of statues, even though they're right beside the person they're most comfortable with
- Not holding a property brochure. Many dedicated buyers won't take a brochure – chances are they've got one already and may have even drawn extension plans all over the back of it
- Standing behind Dad, while Dad puffs his chest out and puts on his best poker face.

This is assuming that the bidder had a plan to start with. This may surprise you, but most buyers don't actually have a top-end figure in mind. Most buyers will 'wait and see', with a vague idea of where to start their bidding but little idea about the 'where to stop the bidding' part of the equation. Determining a bidding strategy while a person with a gavel is screaming at you in a crowded street is a recipe for disaster, particularly if you are new to the bidding game.

This is another reason why bidding success isn't only about budget: not every bidder has a firm plan.

In fact, from Cate's observations, she estimates that around 50 per cent of active bidders have a vague plan, 30 per cent have a firm and adjustable plan, 15 per cent have a firm and non-adjustable plan, and 5 per cent have no plan. Some of this last group probably didn't leave the house that day expecting to buy a property!

People with a vague plan may have a general idea of what they believe to be the property's value, but they won't have a firm upper limit or a designated 'walk away' price. Their assessment of value will most likely be a round number, and they'll probably be quite prepared to have some flex. They will also likely chat to their partner and make bid-increase decisions during the auction. These buyers are more likely to be susceptible to intimidation tactics and to have a change of heart when bidding gets tough.

The 30 per cent who have a firm and adjustable plan will likely bid more strongly and be less impacted by others until the bidding enters their 'non-adjustable' price territory. During the final stages of the auction calls, and particularly when the auctioneer is applying pressure to the two final standing opponents, this category of buyer will be feeling the heat while they try to reassess their price in front of a crowd. If it's a couple bidding, they'll typically have been consultative with each other in the pre-auction days, so the decision to stretch the budget in the face of tough conditions will, most likely, also be consultative. Our observation is that consultation with a partner during an auction usually heightens stress levels for the bidder.

The 15 per cent who have a firm and non-adjustable plan may be nervous, but they'll likely apply and bid to their plan and aren't as likely to be rattled by another bidder. Those who hire professional bidders fit into this category – provided they don't have a bidder who will call them or tempt them to increase their budget during the auction.

The final category, the 5 per cent or so who have no plan, are very unpredictable. After all, someone who buys a house without a plan, a budget, or any intention of buying a property that day are on a different wavelength altogether. They may be impervious to any clever, intimidating bidder tactics because they aren't applying much rationale to what should be a very careful decision.

Considering the number of bidders out there who are nervous, uncomfortable, and don't have a firm, non-adjustable plan, a confident and assertive bidder should absolutely have some degree of impact on the result.

Private sales

Private sales feature in all cities, both capital and regional. While some of the capitals feature plenty of auctions, there is no getting away from private sales. Some properties are advertised outright for private sale with a fixed price. Other properties feature a quoted price range, while some may be listed as 'price on application', or invite 'expressions of interest'.

While these are all private sale campaigns, they differ.

It cannot be assumed that a real estate agent will sell the property to the first person who offers the asking price, either. Agents work for their vendor, and in healthy markets where multiple offers are often fielded from purchasers, agents may pivot the campaign from 'private sale' to a 'best and highest' method (detailed later in this chapter). Occasionally they will facilitate a transparent process such as a simulated auction, where buyers either attend online, in the agency office or at the property.

The challenge with a private sale campaign is that agents aren't bound by specific rules for the methodology that they apply to facilitate the sale. Of course, they can't break the law, but they can determine at any moment when they'd like to apply the various practices I've just mentioned. For buyers, it's not always as straightforward as simply making an offer.

Buyers need to be mindful of the various ways that agents adopt these methods, and they need to be prepared to negotiate.

Negotiating

To begin with, negotiation requires an understanding of the end goal. When purchasing a property, the end goal includes:

- the price
- the terms
- other conditions.

The vendor will usually have a desired amount, but they will also have a 'bottom line'. The two will vary as the days and weeks tick over, and in a moving market, a vendor's expectations may increase with the market movement. If they witness a sale that they consider comparable to their own property, their price expectation could change to reflect this new sale. It's a very precarious practise in a fast-moving market, particularly for agents.

Not all vendors are focused on price, however. Some will have a focus on a sale date, particularly if losses could result. For example, if a vendor has purchased another property and the settlement date is looming, they will likely be particularly motivated to sell by a certain date.

While the end goals are important, equally important are the conditions and challenges that the vendor and the agent are facing. If a buyer has insight into these challenges, they can frame their offers advantageously, and often secure a property quickly and with less buyer competition.

Real estate agents are sometimes under pressure during a sales campaign, and being cognisant of this can give a buyer an edge. Some challenges real estate agents face include:

- a listing authority approaching it's end date
- a vendor who is difficult to deal with
- a competing buyer who is difficult to deal with
- being about to leave their agency.

Sometimes just being nice to the agent can give a buyer an edge.

There is certainly an art to negotiation, and many different tactics can be applied within a negotiation. From time-limited offers to multi-tiered offers, there is an abundance of ways to put an offer forward. Time-limited offers place pressure on an agent and a vendor to either accept or reject within a particular timeframe. This can sometimes backfire, so it's a practise to be careful of when applying. Multi-tiered offers include a series of offers with varying terms: for example, $600,000 with a 30-day settlement period and

$620,000 with a 90-day settlement period. If the vendor is keen for the shorter settlement period, they may take the lower offer. This can be particularly effective when a buyer is aware of the vendor's circumstances.

One of the best tips I can offer buyers when it comes to making offers is to be prepared to sign a contract and leave a small deposit (otherwise known as a 'consideration'). Verbal offers aren't worth anything, nor are they reliable. It's more compelling for a vendor when they see a written offer, even if it is a disappointing offer.

Signing an offer with minimal conditions can also help. Many buyers like the comfort of a finance clause or a building and pest inspection, but in a heated market, these conditions can work against them.

Sometimes during competitive negotiations, all buyers will have a finance clause. This is typical in the more affordable outer-ring areas or first-homebuyer hotspots, but things can get tricky when one or more buyers have *unconditional* offers. An agent will always be hard placed to recommend a 'subject to finance' offer to a vendor over a slightly lower-priced unconditional offer. A finance clause is often acceptable in circumstances like this, but it can be costly if the buyer wants to beat an unconditional offer. For a conditional contract to win the bid, an agent will need to determine with the vendor the value of the unconditional contract in dollar terms in comparison to the subject-to-finance offer.

Some vendors may not be all that sensitive to the idea of the finance clause, but others may have been burnt in the past by sales that didn't proceed, or they could be time-pressed and unwilling to take a chance on re-selling the property if the buyer's finance isn't granted.

Finance clauses present risk to any vendor. We've seen the differential cost buyers anything from a few thousand dollars to over $50,000 when vendors have determined how much higher an offer needs to be for them to accept the contract with the clauses over an unconditional offer. I've often had cases where I've represented the buyer whose lower offer secured the property.

Regional towns are generally more accepting of a finance clause than big cities, and for those buyers who are fortunate enough to encounter an agent who will sell the property to the first offer received at the full asking price, their 'subject to finance' clause won't necessarily cost them a premium or disadvantage them, provided an unconditional buyer doesn't make the same offer at the same time.

We would never suggest that a buyer ignore the advice of their broker or bank, and in some cases buyers indeed need to seek the protection of such a clause, but for a large proportion of buyers there are other ways to seek protection and address risk.

Borrowing money for all asset classes represents risk. Considering the magnitude of the risk and the likelihood of issues occurring should be part of every buyer's process before they clutch onto a blanket finance clause and reduce the number of properties they can target. Being *completely* protected only to miss out on good properties time and time again is upsetting for buyers. In many cases, those who they are missing out to are carrying the same risks.

However, taking a risk with finance when no preapproval has been sought is a dangerous move. All buyers should discuss their approach with their finance provider or broker.

Hre are some other points of advice when negotiating with a real estate agent:

1. Ask the agent for a background on any other offers received, any buyers floating around, and any recent sales that they deem are comparable to the property in question. This will give you an idea of the expectation of price, the competition they're dealing with, and the timeframe that you may need to move within.

2. Upon presenting an offer, you need to be clear with the agent about when you'll likely receive an update from them. This beats calling and sending them messages of desperation. Try to play it cool once you have put your offer forward.
3. Be available for updates. There is nothing worse than missing an important phone call, particularly when a sale has a close-out time.
4. Never tell an agent that an offer is your last offer unless it really is, and even then we don't recommend this. An agent could relay this to another buyer, who could then pip the offer by $1000.
5. Whether you like the selling agent or not, getting them offside can be detrimental. If things are feeling awkward or tempers are rising, stay calm and clear, and remain as respectful as possible. If the negotiation breaks down and becomes unsalvageable, you can resort to contacting the principal of the office, but this should be a last resort.
6. If the negotiation doesn't go to plan, our best advice is to remain as positive with the agent as possible. Sometimes the initial purchaser doesn't complete the sale, and a second chance arises. Other times, the agent may just have a good off-market up their sleeve. (More on off-markets later in this chapter.)

Navigating 'best and highest' and 'expression of interest' sale methods

'Best and highest' sales campaigns are not just restricted to private sales; they can often result when agents receive acceptable offers on properties scheduled for auction, particularly when they have multiple competing bidders to contend with.

'Best and highest' is a format that has been adopted by agents for a long time, and it relates to ascertaining the maximum figure a buyer would be prepared to pay in a situation in which they are blind to other possible offers. A lack of transparency is the issue; the buyers don't know who they're bidding against, and they don't have a figure to beat. All they know is that they only get one opportunity to submit their highest and best offer.

'Best' usually relates to terms. If they know that the vendor is keen on a certain settlement period or a 10 per cent deposit, they can position their offer in the most advantageous way. Unconditional offers – particularly those which are not subject to finance – are favoured by agents and vendors. But the 'highest' part relates to price, and it's the price part that terrifies many.

Buyer's agents don't love this method because it's very difficult to discern the difference between market value and competing interest when a market is running hot. No buyer's agent wants to pay a $50,000 premium for a property that could have been theirs for considerably less, yet they certainly don't want to miss the deal for their client by $500 just for the sake of getting cute with the agent. It's difficult.

Understandably, 'best and highest' is not necessarily the best method. It works for some agents and disappoints for others. The issue is all about transparency versus fear. Fear of missing out (FOMO) is powerful… but the question is whether FOMO is more powerful than the 'herd mentality'.

 ## The power of competiton

I've been working in the property industry since 2003, and I remember the listings I managed as a young agent. I worked tirelessly, opening properties, calling back buyers, meeting new folks on doorsteps, and talking about comparable sales. I often experienced weeks of limited inquires, but as soon as I received an acceptable offer and called all buyers who had requested contracts, I'd have multiple offers. The point is that buyers like a property more when they know that other buyers like it enough to make an offer on it. Moreso, they enjoy knowing that they aren't making a mistake, and popular consensus soothes this fear. It is for this reason that I feel auctions can bring out the strongest results for vendors.

I've seen agents break records with the best and highest method, but I've seen plenty more situations in which auctioned properties have captured buyers' hearts and the results have been 'runaway'. The power of competition and desperation can be intoxicating during an auction, and buyers can stretch to bids that they would never have considered in the cold light of day. The mere thought of someone else's bid validating their 'stretch' budget has spurred many a buyer to bid beyond the realms of what's sensible with regard to a property's value.

The bottom line is that as professional negotiators, good sales agents will know their buyers and recognise the time to call a best and highest process, or default to an open and transparent contest. The message for buyers is to do your due diligence, establish a comparable sales analysis, place a weighting on the pace of the market, and make a firm decision to submit a competitive but realistic final bid.

Being remorseful about losing in a competitive buying situation is always better than overpaying by a large margin. Ask yourself, before bidding, whether your money could purchase another, better-quality property.

'Expressions of interest' is a very similar process to 'best and highest'. In fact, the two can be interchanged depending on the timing and strength of the market.

An 'expressions of interest' process is usually declared at the commencement of a sales campaign, however. It enables buyers to submit offers with varying terms and conditions by a fixed end date, which means that interested buyers have a finite period in which to conduct due diligence and submit their offer. A vendor can then determine which offer appeals the most to them. A vendor who is sensitive to a 'subject to finance' clause, for example, may choose a lower offer that doesn't contain such a clause. Likewise, a vendor may favour a shorter or longer settlement period.

Tackling an expressions of interest campaign requires due diligence, careful pricing analysis, and an awareness of the vendor's preferred terms. Being able to frame an offer with desirable terms will take some of the focus off price. Cate has had plenty of success with offers that weren't necessarily the highest in expressions of interest scenarios.

She'll personally only participate in an 'expression of interest' or 'best and highest' process, however, when her maximum budget represents great value for the property in question. 'Putting it all on the table', so to speak, can be liberating and means you have no regrets.

On using a buyer's agent

People seek the services of a buyer's agent for multiple reasons, including:

- a fear of getting the asset selection wrong
- a fear of missing out on a special property
- a reluctance to deal with selling agents
- time restrictions or holiday/travel plans that clash with a campaign
- avoidance of auctions and auction bidding
- a desire to get a sharper purchase result than they could achieve alone.

This last point is a common driver for prospective clients who contact us. It would be unfair of any buyer's agent to suggest that they could guarantee this, however, particularly in a seller's market.

After all, we may be experienced property negotiators, but we can't control other buyers. We can only outpace them with our due diligence and decision-making, or intimidate them. We can't stop them from participating in a negotiation or cap their budget. There are limits to our negotiating power!

What some people don't place enough emphasis on are the intangible benefits buyer's agents provide, such as:

· deciphering agent-speak
· establishing the facts and the rules of the negotiation
  (yes, there are rules)
· determining a sensible price limit using a science-based
  approach
· identifying any elements of the offer that could influence a
  vendor to accept it
· gleaning more information about the likely competition (such
  as the strength of their last bidding effort and their desired
  terms)
· assisting with conditions of the offer that either strengthen
  the buyer's position or add extra protection when they're
  vulnerable
· conducting thorough and speedy due diligence to ensure that
  the property is exactly what the buyer thinks it is, from zoning
  to easements, covenants to special levies, and so on
· the buyer's agent's preparedness to be vocal when they don't
  like the asset and believe it's an unwise purchase.

Together, these will deliver a buyer a significant negotiating advantage when their competition isn't as well prepared – although they don't ensure a win, or a bargain buy.

Consumers should ask their buyer's agent questions concerning:

· the likely performance of the property in the long term

- the suitability of the property based on their criteria and timeframe
- any perils or pitfalls that the agent's expertise will help them avoid.

For example, our due diligence goes beyond a contract review and a building inspection. We check for nearby council applications and approvals, special levies for capital raising, courtyard leasehold arrangements, social security (DHS) ownership in strata blocks or neighbouring properties, and parking restrictions on the street, among many other things.

 ## Negotiating the negotiation

Frequently, I negotiate with a property's listing agent about *how* the negotiation will go. We negotiate the negotiation, and this is something that few buyers understand, because they aren't familiar with the various processes that take place behind the scenes.

A past negotiation that comes to mind was for a beautiful property that had an auction date set some two weeks ahead. We knew it could be a crowd-pleaser, and the agent and vendor were receptive to early offers. We had a client budget that was not very likely to beat any competition; in fact, their maximum budget was $10,000 shy of the vendor's predetermined reserve. I had to manage a negotiation with the agent that gave us the opportunity to 'get the property on the market' with the budget we had. In other words, the vendor's reserve had to decrease by $10,000 in order for our offer to be considered an acceptable start to the pre-auction bidding.

This was an 'all in or all out' situation for our clients, as they knew that any competition would eliminate them from the race. The negotiation involved a time limit: the agent gave other buyers a whole business day to challenge our offer.

I had to make sure I didn't give the agent the impression that it was my highest bid. Obviously, if an agent knew that, they'd opt to continue working with other buyers and run the campaign for longer. My only chance was that other buyers weren't ready to make offers. I let the agent think that we had another property that was a plan B, and this plan B property was about to sell. We preferred their property (property A) but didn't want to chance missing out on both. So, we put pressure on them to sell their listing to us quickly. As luck had it, the vendor did accept the offer and nobody else bid. Whether it could have sold to us on auction day for the same price or not, we'll never know, but our buyer was relieved to have purchased it prior to auction and without the risk of missing out on future opportunities along the way if this one hadn't worked out.

Time limits can sometimes be very effective, particularly if other potential purchasers are awaiting finance with an auction date in mind (as opposed to being purchase-ready in the event of a pre-auction sale). Often a 24-hour period is insufficient for some, but an experienced buyer will know that an auction date can often be bought forward suddenly, and with short notice.

However, we don't always pounce at the option to secure a property prior to auction. A second example demonstrates this nicely. We were assisting a family with a home purchase and the auction was an online mid-week event. Two weeks prior, we found out the price that we could secure the property for if we chose to pounce early. It seemed a reasonable price and was broadly similar to my own valuation.

Our clients were quite nervous at the thought of someone else securing their dream and asked me to try to secure it prior to the auction. Conversations with the agent confirmed their pre-auction process. Upon receiving an offer, they'd give all interested parties until the close of business the following day. This meant buyers would have well over 24 hours to formulate their position. That's a long time.

I recommended to our clients that we go to auction, knowing that a shorter timeframe, the pressure of auction nerves and the chance of intimidation over a face-to-face Zoom arrangement could deter buyers from stretching their price limits. We secured the property for a good price.

Here's a really interesting third example. The campaign was a private sale with a quoted range, and it became abundantly clear that the vendor's price expectation was rigid at the top end of that range. My appraisal sat at the middle of the quote, so I had some work to do. The agent had to manage a determined vendor, while I was not prepared to budge past the appraised limit.

My task was to find a way to get the agent to agree with me about the value, as opposed to the price. We discussed comparable properties and battled it out and eventually he agreed that he, too, appraised the property at the value I had. I then negotiated with him around how the offer would be presented and treated. There was to be no 'rejection' of the offer. I would only proceed if he would agree to have the vendor countersign the offer and deal exclusively with us. Over the course of two days, we finally secured the property at my appraised price.

There are many steps in the background that agents and offices implement as agency policy when it comes to dealing with offers. They all vary, some have their quirks, and sometimes their protocol is overturned.

Asking questions, understanding the rules, respectfully challenging, and renegotiating is common practice. Negotiating the negotiation is a huge part of what I do.

About bidding wars

If Cate had a dollar for every buyer who has said to her, 'Cate, I don't want to enter into a bidding war', she'd have a lot of full piggybanks. It's an understandable avoidance, particularly for those who've had their hearts set on a property before only to be outbid by someone else's higher offer.

During price downturns or static buying conditions, buyers essentially have it good when it comes to competition. Days on market are longer, auction bidding numbers are lighter, auction clearance rates are lower, and private negotiations are easier.

History has shown us time and time again, though, that Australian property markets eventually recover. Auctions become a bit more competitive, some sale prices are surprisingly strong, private sales move at a quicker pace, and more buyers attend open-for-inspections.

Telling a buyer who has experienced market-trough buying conditions to prepare for competition is hard. The mere idea of someone else coming along with a stronger offer is enough to put many buyers off bidding or participating in the negotiation. 'I'm not interested in a bidding war', they say.

But once a market is strengthening, avoiding bidding wars can cost you a good property.

A bidding war can certainly take the edge off what would have been a bargain buy. Sometimes a bidding war will result in a buyer paying more than they had assessed the market value of the property to be. If we cast our minds back to the heat of the 2021 market, when many cities experienced price growth above 2 per cent per month, the reality was that a $1 million property was growing in value by over $600 per day at this time. Buyers had to be prepared to set the new record with each sale in such a moving market.

The potential cost of avoiding a bidding war is threefold.

Firstly, if the property is particularly special and well-suited to the buyer, the sense of regret once it has sold to someone else could be quite heartbreaking. We often find that in situations where buyers avoid a high-scoring owner-occupier property out of an unwillingness to compete for it, they later look back and feel a strong sense of sadness. They may then compare every future opportunity to the one they let get away, and this can thwart their search going forward.

Secondly, if the market transition has been quick and price growth is gripping, prices could outstrip the buyer's budget and leave them able to afford only lesser-quality or smaller properties.

It's the third cost that is the most expensive long term, however. When buyers actively avoid competition, it often means that they are selecting properties with limited appeal. After all, it makes sense that if a market is heating up and some properties have limited (or nil) buyer interest, they could have some obvious flaws. Maybe the dwelling is on a main road, or perhaps it has a difficult encumbrance or title, or it could have some serious maintenance issues or expensive levies that the new purchaser will have to remedy. Another possibility is that it's overpriced to start with, and no buyers are interested in that particular asset at the vendor's asking price. Not always, but often, a property languishes on the market due to these reasons.

Off-market properties

One of the most dangerous things a buyer can do in an effort to avoid competition is to go on a quest for an off-market purchase, particularly if they aren't prepared to do the due diligence and pricing analysis. At the time of writing, we're experiencing considerably more 'off-market' pitches from agents, whether it be by text, email, or phone call.

Sadly, only a tiny proportion of the off-market properties that agents are peddling are actually good. The vast majority are either compromised, overpriced, or both. If you are currently in the market for a property and receiving agent emails and texts about off-markets, test this theory and have a look at the location and price of each offering. So many are on main roads or in awkward locations. Others have terrible floor plans or poor-quality workmanship. And so many of them are absolutely overpriced.

Why would a vendor sell for a fair (or discounted) price when stock levels are low and buyer appetite is increasing? A truly motivated off-market vendor is usually selling due to a genuine financial need for a swift sale. It may be because they bought an upgrade or downsizer property, and they need to sell their current home in order to manage the settlement. Or, they may be off-loading an investment property with a lease in place, for financial reasons. Sometimes an off-market vendor is tackling a tricky situation, or they require a set of terms that are not mainstream. Whatever the reason, these aren't *opportunistic* sales.

An opportunistic vendor's off-market should be avoided. A pre-market campaign disguised as an 'off-market' is downright dangerous. They can lure buyers in and attract honest offers, only to launch an auction campaign a few weeks later. Vendors and agents then have a firm idea of genuine buyer interest, including the price that interested buyers would be prepared to pay. During this period, buyers are focusing their energy on properties that were never truly off-market to begin with, and likely missing out on exploring other possible options.

Targeting off-market sales just to avoid competing buyers is a terrible solution.

Maximise your chances of winning

The best way to minimise competition is to be decisive and move swiftly when the right property comes along. Sometimes agents will run an auction campaign all the way to auction day, meaning that the chance of competition (and heartache) is higher, but in quite a few situations, buyers can make a firm and fair offer and trigger a sale on an auction property before auction day.

When considering private sales, stealth is the key. Once the due diligence and pricing analysis is complete, a thorough contract review can be quickly organised, and the negotiation can commence quickly. The faster you act, the less time you give other buyers to be attracted to the sales campaign.

A word about buying and selling at the same time

When it comes to moving into their next home, most buyers are faced with the prospect of selling their existing home to make the move. Gone are the days of easy access to bridging finance, and buyers often ask us, 'How do we do this?'

In a stable market, the process is relatively straightforward. The buyers can either choose to sell first and then shop with the security of a known settlement date and a firm deposit in their hand, or they can locate their ideal property and purchase with a long settlement in mind, giving themselves an optimum timeframe to sell.

But when a market is either rising or declining, any buyer who is transitioning from one home to another will be conscious of the impact of a changing market.

In a rising market, the fear for many vendors is that they could sell today and purchase months later when prices are much higher. The value of every dollar could be lower if it takes longer to buy a new property than anticipated. If they choose instead to buy in today's market and then sell afterward, they could sell advantageously, but they put themselves under pressure to meet a particular settlement date. Alternatively, they could settle on the sale before their purchase settles, which would mean sourcing temporary accommodation.

In a declining market, the tables turn the other way. A vendor may choose to sell first and wait it out for their sale to be completed before purchasing in a more opportunistic market. For many though, the temptation to buy as they see sale prices being discounted and days-on-market extending is too great. The advice we give relates to factoring in the impact of a tougher market when it comes time to sell their own home. We lean on conservative sale price estimates.

Battling a sale in a tough period is hard, but battling a sale with a finite settlement date to match is stressful. In other words, the biggest challenge for upgraders, downsizers and those shifting to a new area relates to timing.

It has become very difficult for buyers and sellers to identify where the point of a market shift will be. As they say, 'Nobody rings the bell when the market reaches the bottom'. The only way that we can identify when the market has turned for the better is once prices start to increase again. At that point, we can pinpoint when the market *actually* bottomed out.

When buyers and sellers speculate about the market and try to time an advantageous upgrade, they introduce a new layer of risk. If their expectation of market movement is correct, they will effectively sell at a higher price than they buy at. If their expectation is proved wrong, however, they may find that they have lost some wealth in the trade due to a market fluctuation. If they sell in a down-market and then the market starts to increase while they're shopping, they'll wish they hadn't tried to time the situation after all.

Losing a place on the ladder due to bad timing is never a happy event. The best way to mitigate against this is to time the purchase and sale as concurrently as possible, to trade in the same market. This involves a lot of organisation, and there are lots of elements to consider, such as:

- how to effectively market the property to ensure a prompt sale
- what conservative estimates to rely on when calculating the cost of the 'trade'
- when to start shopping
- how to introduce flexibility into settlement dates
- where to stay if there's a gap between the sale settlement and the purchase settlement.

Cate has helped buyers transition for years, and merging the settlement dates effectively can involve interesting solutions. One family received an offer on their house for a settlement some seven weeks ahead of their purchase settlement date. They were bound for a family holiday around Europe and quite anxious about the prospect of a sooner-than-planned vacate date. Cate told them to pack their things, vacate early, put their belongings in storage for seven weeks, enjoy two nights in a hotel and then fly out with a million dollars in the bank and no mortgage.

More recently, she worked with a lovely couple who were fortunate enough to get a flexible settlement offer on their home. The buyer had enabled them to shop carefully for their next home and had given them the confidence that they could flex within a specified date range when the vendor finally signed a purchase contract.

The process can be intense, but it doesn't have to be stressful.

Key points in this chapter

- Learn to negotiate well on each and every property deal that you do!
- Be decisive and move swiftly when the right property comes along.
- Seek professional help when appropriate. If in doubt, ask!

9

How to build a powerhouse portfolio

The world has endured a tumultuous period since the global financial crisis in 2008, and we've sometimes wondered whether partial ignorance is bliss. After all, had we known of all the potential perils facing the world's major investment banks and financial institutions back then – let alone all the other challenging world events that would take place over the following decades – many of us may have been too fearful to invest in anything ever again! Yet, for all the turmoil, people buying quality assets at sensible prices have enjoyed more than a decade and a half of strong returns.

Thus far in the book, we've looked at the ins and outs of the Buy Right Approach and at how to buy your first property. How do you then take things to the next level? How do you build a powerhouse investment property portfolio?

Use a borrowing-capacity calculator

You drafted your ten-year Buy Right plan back in chapter 3. Pull that plan out again now – it's time to use a borrowing-capacity calculator to run some property investment scenarios.

Many online borrowing capacity calculators exist, and some are better than others. Many of the main banks and second-tier lenders share their own calculators online, but it's important to note that borrowing capacity changes a lot as lender policies change. We like these two calculators, because they take into account multiple lender options and give people a broader idea of their borrowing capacity across multiple lender options:

1. mortgagechoice.com.au/home-loan-calculators/how-much-can-i-borrow/
2. comparethemarket.com.au/home-loans/calculators/borrowing-power-calculator-b/

These calculators are indicative only, and they are designed to give you a broad idea of your borrowing capacity. We recommend a discussion with an experienced mortgage broker to formulate a reliable idea of borrowing capacity. However, if your borrowing capacity looks a bit tight, there are some practical things you can do with your pending investment strategy. You may need to accumulate more equity or savings, or your income may not service the debt that you had initially planned. In this latter case, focusing on a less expensive property, combined with seeking a stronger rental return, could make the difference between borrowing now or waiting it out.

In chapter 10, we look at financing and some important points about ownership structures which will affect your borrowing capacity.

Keep it simple, stupid (KISS)

The legendary investor Peter Lynch of Fidelity once said that he liked to invest in businesses that even an idiot could run, because sooner or later, one will. There's a great deal to be said for this as a philosophy for both business and investment: the more complexity and moving parts there are to a strategy, the greater the chance of something going wrong.

There's no need to make your portfolio plan too clever, or to make processes harder than they need to be. Philosopher Henry David Thoreau said, 'Simplify, simplify, simplify' – and in that spirit, here are six ways to keep your financial plan simple:

1. **Set goals.** While plans tend to change over time, it helps to have an end goal to work towards so that you can begin with the end in mind. You thought through your financial and non-financial aims in chapter 2: refer back to them to keep yourself on track.

2. **Plan for all seasons.** All asset classes, property included, come in and out of favour and experience summer and winter seasons. Plan to invest through both the good and bad times.

3. **Diversify.** Don't put all your eggs in one basket, or one property. Ensure, too, that you're taking advantage of investments outside property where this may make financial sense for you, especially in superannuation. A great financial planner can help you get the balance right here.

4. **Have a clear plan.** Know how many properties you need to invest in to meet your goals. Invest when you can, and don't try to time the market.

5. **Don't rely on timing.** It makes sense to buy low and sell high as best you can, of course, but try not to worry too much about market timing. It's time in the market that's your friend.

6. **Manage risks and think long term.** Invest, don't gamble, and take a long-term view.

Naturally we could go into more depth here, but that would probably defeat the point! Apple's co-founder Steve Jobs noted that it takes time and effort to get your thinking clean and clear enough to keep things simple, but the effort to do so is well worth it, because once you get there you can move mountains.

EQ, AQ and long-term investing

Do you need to be clever to invest well? Well… no, not really! We can probably all remember peers from our schooldays who took academic achievement in their stride, yet couldn't easily deal with social situations, and in some instances could barely tie their own shoelaces. An intelligence quotient, or 'IQ', is a traditional measure of intelligence based upon standardised aptitude tests, but while a single number might indicate something useful about raw ability, it has limitations in terms of measuring behaviour.

The good news for budding investors is that while a high IQ is useful for identifying and understanding a strategy, it's far from the sole determinant of success. An average IQ might even be helpful if it means that you retain humility. Warren Buffett famously said that 'investing is not a game where the guy with the 160 IQ beats the guy with a 130 IQ. Rationality is essential'.

An emotional quotient, or 'EQ', can be critical – especially for people (particularly young men, it has to be said) who are prone to excitement, chasing the latest fad and taking big risks. And, since every investor will experience market corrections, downturns, and times when things just won't go right, an ability to deal with adversity ('AQ') is at least as important too. As heavyweight boxing champion Mike Tyson once said, 'Everyone has a plan 'til they're punched in the mouth'. Investors don't necessarily need to be too creative ('CQ'), however, since it's possible to learn from the successes and failures of others' strategies.

Overall, all you need is a solid strategy, the discipline to stick to it, and the mental fortitude to keep going when times get tough.

To conclude with Buffett again, 'What is needed is a sound intellectual framework for making decisions and the ability to keep emotions from corroding that framework'. As the adage goes, investment is simple, though it's not always easy!

As an investor, you can't control the returns you achieve, so you have to focus on the process – continually improving, learning from mistakes, and refining your skills. Buy at sensible prices and limit the downside. Prices will rise and fall through market cycles, but if you avoid buying in periods of wild exuberance, this will help to manage the risks. You can't control your luck, but you can resolve to maximise the opportunities afforded to you through life. Oh, and give those casinos a wide berth!

Don't just do something: stand there

Patience in property investment and building your net worth isn't just a virtue – it's essential. In the short-term markets can appear risky, but over the long term they tend to be much less so.

Try not to fall in love with an investment property – it won't love you back. Spread your risk, sit back, and enjoy the enormous power of compound growth.

The way to spread your risk is by diversifying your investments. Some may argue that this requires investing in multiple other asset classes (such as shares), but we think of this as diversifying your properties. This may include a mix of price points or states and territories. What we don't recommend is purchasing multiple similar properties in one city or township. Markets don't move in synchronicity, and many experienced investors (including us) could describe to you the merits of holding diversified properties across multiple states and territories.

In cricket, experienced batters don't get too excited when they make a great score; and, correspondingly, they don't get too despondent or punish themselves when they go through a rough trot. Similar principles apply to the building of long-term wealth. Try not to be too emotional or bemoan challenges, as this can send you off-track. Provided you have a sensible, long-term strategy, adverse or very strong performance over the short term shouldn't faze you too much.

You can remove emotions from investing by adopting a long-term view:

- **Buy quality assets you never need to sell.** Clearly, nobody intends to buy poor-quality assets, but some are much riskier than others, and, yes, diversification helps.

- **Check prices infrequently.** The internet has made it very easy (too easy!) to find comparable property prices – try to switch off the market and background noise and use different timeframes to review your performance. An annual review may be enough.

- **Think of investments as great assets and businesses.** Prices will always fluctuate, but thinking of your portfolio in terms of its quality rather than in dollar terms can help you to tune out the markets.

- **Read classic investment books.** While specifics change, the fundamentals of successful investing tend to remain constant over time, and reading the classics is a good way to remind yourself of how and why this is true.

There are many patient investors out there with some terrific resources available, too – these can be an effective 'support group' for you, so go and find them! You don't have to be particularly smart; you just have to be patient.

Pete was intrigued by the game of chess for some years when he was at junior school. One of the interesting things about chess is that when it's your turn, you're obliged to move, even when your interests would be served best by doing nothing. This is the unenviable situation known as 'zugzwang'. Thankfully, in the real world we aren't always compelled to move, and sometimes inaction is the right choice.

Organisations tend to be loaded with people that believe doing something is better than doing nothing. 'It didn't work out, but at least we tried' can be an enduring refrain. However, being calm and thoughtful instead of maniacally active can mean that you make more rational and less emotional decisions, even if in the short term it means having to put your reputation or credibility on the line. Taking a 'wait and see' approach can often serve you better than doing something immediately just because you can.

In investing, as we've seen, buying and selling quality assets too often has a hugely detrimental effect on returns, due to transaction costs, capital gains taxes, and often, poor timing. Yet the need to *do something* seems to plague many investors, especially men. If you have this trait, consider setting up a 'fun account' – a share-trading account containing 5 to 10 per cent of your net worth, for entertainment purposes.

One of the greatest advantages that an investor has over a chess player is that there's no compulsion to move. Get clear on your own strategy, and when there's nothing to do... do nothing. Buy, renovate, and hold – this simple strategy really works!

Choose your endgame

At various points in the book, we've mentioned selling ('divesting') property. While the Buy Right Approach is about buying and holding for the long term, selling property can be part of your overall strategy. As Pete mentioned in chapter 1, selling properties in retirement, for example, is a common endgame among property investors: he may do this himself. And remember 'Anna', from chapter 7? She purchased two investment properties as a rent-vestor, then sold one of these properties to fund the purchase of her own home.

A long-term property investment strategy underpins the Buy Right Approach. Yet it's also important to consider and choose between two sub-strategies: buy and hold forever, or divest and reinvest?

A 'divest and reinvest' endgame involves divesting some or all of your property assets and using the funds to invest in other asset classes, such as shares. If you choose this strategy, you'll most probably focus on properties that can outperform the market in terms of their capital growth, and you'll be less concerned about rental returns.

With a 'buy and hold forever' approach, by comparison, rental return is crucial. Ideally, you'll want all of your properties to be 'unencumbered' (paid off) and delivering rental income by the time you retire. This means you need to plot out your acquisitions to make sure you have a cashflow that will not only enable you to continue acquiring property, but will also help you to pay down all of the debt. Note that it can be hard to achieve both strong growth and strong yield, so if you're aiming for a blend of both, you may have to settle for more moderate growth and yield.

 Buy and hold forever, or divest and reinvest

Let's look at examples of the two approaches.

An investor client of mine chose the 'divest and reinvest' approach. They purchased a gorgeously renovated Victorian terrace house in Melbourne's inner north for $1.325 million and rented it out for $750 per week. The property is tipped to deliver strong capital growth returns, but the rental returns won't break any records.

In fact, the cashflow shortfall associated with this property will be considerable; it's all about that very strong expected growth.

If the client pays both principal and interest on their loan, and utilises offset accounts effectively, they should be able to pay off the loan within 25 years, possibly sooner. Only at this point will they have an unencumbered property that's delivering them a rental return. The property will, however, become cashflow neutral (that is, break even) at some point before this. For many capital cities it's typically after around 12 to 15 years of ownership that rents will have risen enough to cover the mortgage repayments and other costs (such as rates and land tax). However, for regional assets, the period of time to achieve neutral cashflow is often much less, because rental yields tend to be stronger in regional areas.

If they have multiple properties like this in their portfolio, it's likely that they won't be able to pay down all their debt across the portfolio before retirement. And it's likely that for them, as for many investors, that's OK. They'll divest one, some, or all their properties when they retire, pay the capital gains tax bill, and likely reinvest the profits for a post-retirement income.

Those who rely heavily on their properties' rental income to cover loan repayments, of course, need to take heed of the fact that selling a positively geared property will actually reduce their borrowing capacity, since it will reduce their overall income. This is not so important in retirement when they're no longer acquiring properties, but it's an important consideration prior to that.

The canvas looks quite different for an investor whose preferred strategy is to buy and hold forever. One young investor I worked with purchased his second property in North Geelong in 2019 – a neatly renovated 1970s two-bedroom villa unit with a small courtyard in a great street. He purchased for $350,000 and rented it out immediately after settlement for over $370 per week. The property was immediately cashflow neutral, and subsequent rental increases tipped it into positive cashflow territory. He intends to keep the property permanently as a source of rental income.

With a 'buy and hold forever' approach, having enough cashflow to maintain and add to your portfolio is the primary consideration. Investors also need to carefully consider factors such as:

- each property's maintenance requirements
- each property's tenant demographic
- the long-term outlook for each property and location
- overall portfolio diversification
- tax implications.

Of course, these should be considered by 'divest and reinvest' investors too. But if, for example, you were planning to sell a particular property in 15 years, the fact that it will (let's say) likely need a full renovation in 18 to 20 years' time has different implications than it would if you were planning to continue to hold it.

It's important to have your chosen approach front of mind when reviewing your investments. All too often we help an investor map out a portfolio tailored to their bigger picture, only to have them lose sight of their own strategy. Some capital-growth-oriented, 'divest and reinvest' clients will come back to us a year or so later to complain that their gross rental returns are less than a friend's – yet they chose an aggressive capital-growth strategy, whereas their friend opted for a yield-oriented, 'buy and hold forever' strategy.

Conversely, an investor who chose a 'buy and hold forever' strategy and has enjoyed the fruits of their decision in the form of optimised cashflow and positive rental returns may come to us lamenting the fact that their property has not grown in value at the rate that other properties have. We always remind them of their initial strategy and the reasons that they chose it. The question to ask when assessing your results is always: is the property delivering what you asked of it?

Also, as we've said before, property is a long game. Give your strategy enough time to work!

When to stop purchasing

When you're planning your portfolio, always keep your endgame in mind.

Too many budding investors get carried away with acquiring more and more properties, and forget about their 'how much is enough' figure. As their income rises, so does their borrowing capacity, and it may be easy to just keep adding properties to the portfolio. What they often overlook, however, is the burden that a property can represent when they're approaching retirement.

If you're planning to 'buy and hold forever', you may need to work for many years after each purchase to fund the repayments. Your property portfolio can then leave you feeling trapped on a corporate or business treadmill, working hard to pay down your debt while everyone else around you is retiring.

 Resist the temptation to buy when you don't need to

I started my property journey early in life, but I did fall prey to buying more property in my forties when it wasn't necessary to achieve my goals. These days, when temptation strikes (which happens a lot!), I resist it. I remind myself that every acquisition takes more time to pay down, and time becomes precious as I step closer to retirement.

Keep reviewing how much is enough for you – and pay particular attention to when you think you may want to retire, do something different, or have the choice to stop working. Over-achieving your financial goals may be exciting, but it costs your future self *time*.

In the next chapter, we explore financing your portfolio – the final, critical piece of the investment puzzle – in more detail.

Key points in this chapter

- For most average investors, a simple strategy can be best.
- When working out your strategy, try to begin with the end in mind – what's your long-term ambition or likely endgame?
- Buy, renovate, and hold property for the long term.
- Picking the right properties is one important skill – discipline and patience are just as important!

10

Financing

Financing! It's said that property is a game of financing with houses in the middle, and there's a good deal of truth in that. If you can't borrow, it becomes very difficult to keep building a portfolio, so it makes sense to map out the best borrowing strategy that you can.

Before 2007, it was possible for individual investors to rack up huge mortgage debts. These days, there's a limit to how much debt you can have, which is normally based upon a multiple of your income – for example, five or six times your total income, including a portion of your rental income. That means you need to use every dollar of your available borrowing capacity wisely.

In the previous chapter, you calculated your borrowing capacity and ran some numbers on your Buy Right plan. Now, let's get into the nitty-gritty of how to finance your property portfolio.

Refinancing and ownership structures

Refinancing refers to resetting a loan. This can be done with the same lender, but it is mostly conducted with a new lender. This is how people finance a lot of their investment purchases after the first property, rather than always saving deposits. Refinancing enables the borrower to increase their mortgage size based on the growth in value of the existing property. For example, if a $600,000 purchase four years ago is now valued by a bank at $700,000, the borrower will have $100,000 in additional equity that they can access for the purposes of a deposit for a subsequent purchase.

Refinancing is essentially the same process as getting your first loan, but sometimes the paperwork is not as extensive if you are refinancing with the same lender. We recommend that investors talk to their strategic mortgage broker about identifying the best loan option for their investment strategy.

Loan structuring is a vital consideration, whether it be a discussion about principal and interest versus interest only, buffer accounts, offset accounts, tax deductibility, cross-collateralisation, or other elements such as professional packages.

Borrowers may also have other lending challenges that need the advice of a strategic mortgage broker. Challenges can include income types, ownership structures, offshore employment, parental leave, and work contract end dates, among many others. There are many important aspects to understand and discuss before leaping into the cheapest loan products.

We have met too many investors who have made tiny mistakes with their lending choices that have cost them tens of thousands of dollars over time. A common mistake is to avoid an offset account. People confuse 'redraw' and 'offset', yet they are not the same thing. Redraw may be cheaper, but it undermines an investor's ability to claim optimal tax deductions; offset, on the other hand, enables this and offers flexibility and choice throughout the investor's journey.

Getting the right advice at the start from an investment-savvy, strategic mortgage broker is imperative.

Can you truly afford it?

Before you do any preparation, searching or shortlisting, ask yourself whether a purchase is actually feasible for you *right now*. Many professional buyers or finance brokers will tell you that that there's no better time to buy than when you can afford it, but that's the key – you have to be able to afford it!

Using debt magnifies both your gains and your losses. So you need to manage debt carefully, and always have a repayment plan in place.

Are you sure you'll be able to comfortably afford the repayments into the future? Obviously life can be unpredictable, but make sure you're not ignoring foreseeable risks. Maybe your job or business is insecure in some way. Maybe you have plans that could result in a reduction of your income.

Be very cautious about predicting increases in your income, too. You may be confident that an imminent pay rise or income change will springboard you into being able to afford more debt. Don't be hasty. Aim to listen to your head over your heart!

Sometimes it's wiser to look at purchasing a more affordable property. Pete had to choose this route after quitting his corporate career to start his own businesses, and it can work well. However, not if 'affordable' translates to a 'compromised' property! In this case, it's better to wait until you have the equity or funds to make a less compromised, longer-term purchase.

A compromised property is a property that buyers and banks don't like. Compromises include poor or undesirable locations, internal structural issues, and environmental threats. Whatever the compromise, it will downgrade the property's capital growth potential, or its rental potential. At worst, it could prevent a buyer from getting their preferred loan product.

Let's take a closer look at some of the things banks don't like in a property.

Do the banks like this property?

Often buyers will tell us that their finance is fine. 'Oh, that's no issue. My bank is happy to lend me $X million!' It can come as a rude shock when they realise that, while they may be an idyllic borrower, their chosen property is less than ideal.

Even when Cate's clients are nonchalant about buying unconditionally (whether it be at auction or on a private sale contract), she still scrutinises the asset herself. She tells her clients, 'Cate doesn't like properties which the banks don't like'.

The list of unsuitable and undesirable properties is longer than most borrowers can imagine – whether it be a property type that lenders don't want to secure their capital against, a building or area that a lender considers itself 'overexposed' to, a local government zone that's unsuitable for residential lending, or a title type that is deemed to be higher risk. Not only will such properties be difficult to finance, they'll also add a lot of risk to your portfolio – because they'll most likely be challenging for others to finance too, and therefore difficult to sell.

Minimum internal floor area restrictions can strike for many apartment buyers. The rules often change, but most lenders are consistent with their minimal floor area rules. Some lenders will deem a security property acceptable if the internal floor area is 45 square metres (not counting balcony, eaves, or car space). Some will accept car spaces as part of the total area, but could demand a minimum total of 50 square metres.

And just when we think that we have a lender's rules figured out, they can apply a postcode overlay. For example, some lenders will tolerate a 35-square-metre internal floor area – but not in specific postcodes. For apartments in the red-flag postcodes, the acceptable minimum figure could be 50 square metres.

To put this into perspective, many studio apartments range from 20 to 32 square metres in size; many one-bedroom apartments hover around 35 to 40 square metres in size, and many older style, boutique two-bedroom apartments are around 60 to 70 square metres in size. A buyer can't be certain of their one-bedroom apartment floor area without a reliable floor plan showing measurements. Cate always carries a laser measure in her glovebox for such tasks.

 ## Four troublesome lending scenarios

I recall in my loan-writing days as a mortgage broker four other stand-out, troublesome scenarios that caused a stir for my clients, who were unaware of the issues they'd face when loan assessment time approached.

The first scenario was a title issue. As rare as they are, Melbourne's tightly held inner south-eastern suburbs of Elwood, St Kilda, Balaclava, and Ripponlea are often plagued with the curse of the 'company share title': instead of a freehold or strata title, which confers ownership of the individual property on the purchaser, each owner possesses shares in a company that owns the entire building. This title type dates from the early 20th century when Art Deco reigned. Sadly, many buyers are dazzled by this beautifully stylish era, and forget to ask about title. Most banks won't lend beyond 60 per cent for this type of title; only a few offer an 80 per cent loan-to-value ratio (LVR). A buyer with less than a 20 per cent deposit may therefore find themselves in trouble if they don't do their homework.

Many years ago, I inspected a neat and tidy villa unit in Melbourne's Moonee Ponds that was soon to be auctioned. The agent hadn't yet received the contract from the vendor's solicitor, and knowing my values in the area, I discussed the likely price tag of the property with her. Diplomatically, she indicated that it would be likely to exceed $460,000; I knew as well as she did that $480,000 was a more probable price given its finish, land size and location. Anyway, the contract didn't arrive until the Thursday night before the auction. To everyone's horror, it was a company share title.

Buyers would need between a 20 and 40 per cent deposit, depending on their lender's policy on company share units – this blow knocked out all but one buyer, and the unit sold for $407,000 with no competition.

Number two in the 'memorable loan application' stakes was a beautiful rural property in a small postcode that had unfortunately been deemed a fire risk: the Black Saturday bushfires of 2009 had struck the area, and this postcode was on a 'postcode restricted list' with many lenders.

The third troublesome finance application that I juggled applied to a flood-damaged property that a client had set her sights on. Her trade-qualified brother had encouraged her to pursue the property, knowing that he could add immense value by fixing the damage. However, the valuer's risk rating eliminated it as an option. The bank was not interested in funding the purchase under any circumstances.

Fire and flood-damaged properties may seem lucrative, but they are fraught with danger when it comes to lender appetite. Likewise, condemned properties, those without adequate kitchen facilities, and those in a state of semi-construction or semi-renovation can present problems for borrowers. I recall a situation when friends purchased a rustic Victorian single-fronted cottage with a near nonexistent kitchen: they had to approach multiple lenders and experienced settlement delays due to the difficulty of getting finance.

The fourth and worst scenario I've witnessed was when a lender determined that there were insufficient comparable sales in the area to support the price on the contract. I actually witnessed this scenario twice during my mortgage-broking years. In both cases, the client had done nothing wrong, and the price was fair and reasonable based on historical sales, yet the lender's policy stipulated that three comparable property sales within a three-month period needed to be sighted by a valuer for the loan approval to proceed.

Zoning

Zoning, and the difference between commercial and residential lending, is another issue that's vital for buyers to understand. A bank is likely to categorise a regular house in a regular residential street as a residential loan security. It's when you have a unit that sits in a commercial zone; or above, next to, or behind a commercial space; or when the property has commercial character that things can get murky.

Some properties may look and feel like residences, but issues can strike if they are 'caretaker residences' – that is, they serve as a residence for a business owner who runs the conjoined premises commercially. A property doesn't have to be commercially zoned to be considered commercial. Also, a lender may not necessarily determine that a commercial dwelling is ineligible for a residential loan.

 Some case studies of zoning issues

I once had a client who was interested in a home at the rear of an old shop. The house was residentially zoned, but the valuer deemed it a commercial property for the purpose of the loan. As a result, my client was no longer eligible for residential loan rates, terms, or fees. The higher commercial lending interest rate, combined with the shorter 15-year loan term, meant that he couldn't service the proposed debt.

The rules around zoning aren't always clear, but there are usually tell-tale signs that trouble could raise its ugly head. With many other potential issues, I'll highlight the risks or encourage the buyer to investigate the implications of a particular choice, but I'm black and white about zoning. Residential zoning versus commercial zoning can make the difference between financing a purchase and losing the deposit completely. The trouble that certain zones can represent for buyers who have residential preapproval cannot be underestimated.

A residential loan preapproval means just that: *the bank must consider the purchase to be a residential dwelling.* Finding out whether a property is residentially zoned (or otherwise) isn't hard. Every single contract will mention the zoning; asking a lawyer or conveyancer to point it out is a simple matter.

I once had a buyer who was enquiring about a house on a busy road with a few industrial workshops in the immediate vicinity. The appeal of the property was the price tag – it seemed too good to be true. The issue was the zone. This buyer wasn't able to fund a 30 to 40 per cent deposit on commercial lending terms.

In the same week, a lovely young first homebuyer called with a different zoning enquiry. The property he'd found was not only selling off the plan (already enough to make me anxious), but was also in a high-rise block above shops in a commercial zone. He told me a few times that it wasn't a commercial-flavoured unit, and kept coming back with questions and objections: 'But what if it's an obvious apartment?' 'But the agent said I just need 10 per cent.' 'But what about if I ask another bank?' I pointed out the risk and said, 'I can't endorse it. All I can do is tell you why it's a *no* for me'.

Banks may consider an apartment above a shop to be a residential dwelling, but if it's zoned as commercial and the property is purchased unconditionally at auction, it comes with the significant risk that the bank may decide to enforce the commercial lending terms based on the property being a commercial security. This means, as stated earlier, that the buyer may need a 30 to 40 per cent bank deposit (as opposed to 5 to 10 per cent), and commercial lending rates will apply. These are generally higher than residential interest rates, and the loan term may be shorter. Unless the buyer has significant emergency funds on tap, they won't be able to meet the loan requirements. They'll rescind the purchase, forfeit their deposit, and pay the vendor for losses, and they may also potentially be sued.

Even if the bank decides to finance the property based on it being residential (provided other residential policy requirements are met), the buyer will potentially face problems when they come to sell the property, as another lender may decide to consider it a commercial security, or policy may have tightened. If other properties in the building are sold later and the resultant sale prices are low due to buyer nerves or inability to obtain residential finance, the valuation will remain low too.

A mixed-use zone might be acceptable to a particular lender for one buyer, yet may be rejected by that same lender for another buyer. Lender and mortgage insurer appetite for a given type of property always takes into consideration their overall exposure to it, too, and inner-city suburbs are often quite densely populated with mixed-use dwellings.

The same caution can apply to properties in formerly commercial or industrial areas that are in the process of gentrifying. Zoning can be integral to the future use of an area, its development potential, the surrounding streetscape, and exciting changes in store. Zones aren't to be feared, but should always be understood.

There are many zone types; be crystal clear about what zoning your preapproval covers. A residential loan product can cover other zone types, but usually this is at the bank's discretion, and both the valuer's report and the borrower's loan-to-value ratio (LVR) will be taken into consideration.

A higher LVR will generally spell higher scrutiny. In most cases, loan amounts above 80 per cent will mean that lenders mortgage insurance (LMI) applies, and often, the mortgage insurer assesses the loan application as well as the lender. In most cases, the mortgage insurer is even stricter than the lender.

Lenders mortgage insurance

Lenders mortgage insurance (LMI) plays a huge role in the loan application process. What a lender may agree to, a mortgage insurer could baulk at. In fact, in many cases, the lenders mortgage insurer has the last – and most critical – say. The relationship is interesting.

Many borrowers falsely believe that LMI protects them, but that's not the case: LMI is solely to protect the lender, not the borrower.

LMI is required if the lender considers the loan amount to carry sizeable risk. In most cases this risk sits at 80 per cent LVR, but it can vary depending on the loan type, the borrower's credentials, and the security property. For 'low-doc' (low-documentation) loans, for instance, which carry a higher risk, a lender might set a lower LVR threshold for LMI.

The borrower pays a one-off premium upon settlement of the property, calculated on a sliding scale based on the total funding as a percentage of the property value (LVR). This premium often comes as a shock, and can blow out into the tens of thousands of dollars. A 95 per cent borrower, for example, may pay 3 per cent of the property purchase price in LMI; for a $700,000 purchase, this would equate to $21,000. The premium can often be capitalised onto the loan, however (in other words, added to the base loan and amortised over the entire loan period).

It's worth noting that some bank employees, medical professionals and high-net-worth clients may be eligible for loans of up to 90 per cent LVR without LMI being required.

Some might define the LMI step as the most highly scrutinised part of the loan-application process, and we've seen plenty of situations where the bank says yes and the insurer says no. However, if the bank likes the property enough to finance it to 95 per cent – or, better still, likes it enough also to offer capitalised LMI – then we can rest assured that one important step in the process has been covered off.

And for many buyers, LMI provides an opportunity to buy at today's prices, rather than being forced to keep saving and risk being 'priced out' of the properties they want.

Valuation shortfall risk

The term 'valuation shortfall' is dreaded by all. What does it mean? It's a banking term which means that the bank valuation is less than the price paid for a property. This is a rare occurrence; nonetheless, it's something that every buyer should be mindful of and prepared for.

Valuation methods vary based on the lender's and borrower's circumstances. Buyers who are borrowing at a level which places them into LMI territory need to be particularly aware of the process that their lender will be following post-sale. Typically, as mentioned already, LMI is applicable above 80 per cent borrowings. For some lenders, the difference between 80 per cent and 90 per cent borrowings can translate to a full valuation being required, as opposed to a kerbside or automated (computer-modelled) valuation. A full valuation will also be ordered, in most cases, if an automated valuation suggests an anomaly, and a valuer will physically attend the property to conduct the valuation.

When a valuation shortfall strikes, the outcomes can range from moderately stressful to dire. It doesn't necessarily spell disaster, and the buyer won't automatically lose the property, but they will generally have to cough up extra money. Many private sale purchases have finance clauses, hence the borrower's deposit is protected if they have to exit the contract with a finance clause not being met; with auctions, though, the borrower has to manage the shortfall themselves or risk losing their deposit.

Let's look at an example. Say that you purchase a property for $600,000 on a 90 per cent LVR, and the property is later valued by the lender at $550,000 – a shortfall of $50,000. You have a few options:

- If the lender is prepared to fund 90 per cent of the property's value, this becomes $495,000, or 90 per cent of the valuation of $550,000 – as opposed to the $540,000 you were expecting when you purchased the property for $600,000. You'll need to come up with the difference – an additional $45,000 on top of your original $60,000 (10 per cent) deposit.

- If you're eligible for increased borrowings, you could reapply for a loan with a higher LVR. However, most lenders are tough on increased LVRs, and most property buyers are capped at a maximum of 95 per cent. Your pool of potential lenders at this LVR is much more limited. In this example, even on a 95 per cent lending basis, your maximum loan amount would be $522,500 (95 per cent of $550,000), which still leaves a shortfall of $27,500. You'd also need to pay an increased LMI premium.

- If you're confident that the valuer has it wrong, there are channels you can go through to contest the valuation. However, it's fair to say that most valuers won't roll over easily if someone outside the profession challenges their work.

Some buyers are fortunate enough to have access to other borrowed funds, sometimes through equity and other times through parental and family loans. If a buyer can't complete the purchase, however, they face 'rescission'. This means that the contract is voided, and that the vendor and agency retain the deposit, and can potentially sue the purchaser for any losses caused to the vendor. This is grim, but very rare.

So, what mitigating steps can buyers can take to protect themselves from the financial upset and personal angst of a valuation shortfall? There are three:

1. The first and most obvious is to be well-informed at the time of setting a price limit or formulating an offer. Do your due diligence! You need to have confidence that the price you're offering is fair and reasonable, and not an overpayment. (Obviously, there's a fine line to negotiate here between conservative and competitive.) Great preparation is particularly important if your LVR is over 80 per cent or you're purchasing off the plan.
2. Next, you need to think like a valuer. If very few comparable properties have been sold in the area in the recent past, that could spell trouble. You need to think about what other recent sales data a valuer could draw on to support a valuation.
3. The final step is to have a contingency plan if you're concerned that the property's price tag could be scrutinised. This could come in a few forms: you could have a 'war chest' of savings as a buffer, an available loan or line of credit, kind family members, an alternative lender option, the availability of a higher LVR loan, or an 'out clause'.

'Out clauses' are contract terms such as 'subject to satisfactory valuation' or 'subject to finance'. Unfortunately, at auction, it's nearly impossible to have an out clause in place; committed buyers need to take an educated leap and back themselves in the bidding process. Buyers can also take comfort from the fact that many capital-city properties do sell at auction and all buyers are in the same boat. For a private sale or post-auction negotiation, however, buyers who are nervous can consider a 'subject to satisfactory valuation' or 'subject to finance' clause.

Example of a 'subject to satisfactory valuation' condition at work

In 2017, I faced a valuation shortfall situation with a dear client. We'd made a move to purchase an attractive investment property prior to auction, and my comparable sales analysis indicated high fours was an appropriate value. After submission of a contract for $480,000, negotiations with the vendor resulted in agreement at $487,000 – a fair price (or so I thought). I knew that my client didn't wish to buffer any shortfall, and I felt protective of their interests, so I included a 'subject to satisfactory valuation' condition in the contract. This meant that when the bank valuation came back at $460,000, we were able to walk away from the purchase.

Here's the twist: the property proceeded to auction and sold under the hammer a few weeks later for $485,000! A valuation is all about perception: one person's idea may not necessarily align with another's.

Valuation of off-the-plan properties

Scrutiny increases somewhat for off-the-plan properties, and if you enter an unconditional off-the-plan contract without a contingency plan, you're putting yourself at risk.

Generally, too, bank valuations of off-the-plan properties will not take place until the property is ready for settlement. In some cases, this can be two or three years after you sign the contract – you're betting on a property sale price in a future market. It's a pure gamble. As such, these purchases deserve caution and, of course, a contingency plan.

About comparable sales data

While it may seem ridiculous, as we touched on earlier, when limited comparable sales data is available, a loan application can be thrown into jeopardy with some lenders. Banks prefer their panel valuers to generate a minimum number of comparable sales that have not only sold within a recent, defined period but have also settled.

'Comparable' is a term that is bound by a number of variables. These include:

- a land size variation of no greater than 20 per cent
- a character and size (floor area, style, number of bedrooms, and so on) that is considered a close match
- a timeline that is tight enough to draw a reasonable comparison.

As mentioned earlier, Cate twice experienced situations during her mortgage broker days when the lender rejected the property based on insufficient comparable sales. It wasn't that the property was bad or the price was too high; it was merely a case of the valuer's report having an insufficient number of comparable sale properties and the lender not being able to tick that box.

About minimum rental return conditions

One final point to note about valuations: most investment loan preapprovals are based upon a minimum rental return to the investor. The condition will usually be evident in the preapproval letter conditions and will either be represented with a percentage gross yield figure or a weekly rental amount. If the bank valuer's rental appraisal doesn't match the agency appraisal, you may have a problem. It's always advisable to obtain a rental appraisal figure from a valuer.

*

Overall, borrowing capacities are not as high as they used to be. Therefore, it's important to have a borrowing strategy, and to make sure that you make the best possible use of every dollar of borrowing power that you have.

If you can avoid the key pitfalls we have outlined and adopt a long-term approach, then you should create significant equity and wealth over time. Much time can be spent working out the perfect 'endgame' strategy, but in our experience the most important thing is to build the equity in the first place. Circumstances can change over time, and sometimes life gets in the way of best laid plans, but if you can create a pool of equity for your retirement then this will ensure that you have a wide range of choices in your later years.

Key points in this chapter

- Getting the right advice at the start is imperative.
- There's no better time to buy than when you can afford it – but you have to be able to afford it!
- It's important to have a borrowing strategy that makes the best possible use of every dollar of borrowing power that you have.

11

Navigating the future

The world will change over time. That's OK! And it's inevitable. You will change too! That's also inevitable, and not a bad thing. Let's have a think about what has changed over the decades, and the future of property investment.

 Cate looks back

I was born in Melbourne's northern suburbs, but my parents had dreams of moving to the coast, and we moved to Sorrento when I was in kindergarten. Dad quit his corporate job and took on a new business, which was incredibly brave. Mum kept a toe in nursing, but gave up the big Melbourne hospitals to work at a geriatric ward in Rosebud – a backwards career step for her which she may have been sad about taking.

Back then, Sorrento was comparatively cheap. Our dirt road had 33 dwellings, almost all of which were locked up throughout the year, inhabited only in summertime by Toorak-based visitors. The old money still exists in Sorrento today, but the suburb's popularity has gone through the roof, and its median house price is far higher than that of Melbourne.

I remember our Sorrento house being built. We stayed in a very basic little two-bedroom flat above my uncle's shop on Nepean Highway in Rosebud for the year and drove to Sorrento almost daily to see the builder's progress. When the house was finished and we moved in, Mum stuck old bedsheets to the window frames with drawing pins as curtains. We used furniture borrowed from family members for quite a while.

Housing preferences and needs have changed so much! Our kind of 'move-in ready' was typical for 1979; today, 'move-in ready' includes window furnishings – along with landscaping, kitchen appliances and even TVs.

For years after we moved in, too, we didn't holiday or go out for dinners. Mum kept the house humming, however, and back-to-back dinner parties were not unusual. We kids would be fed and sent to bed early and would hear the grown-ups downstairs enjoying Mum's cooking.

I could gauge the profitability of my dad's business by the amount of discounted food Mum bought. Packs of sausages with 'red spot special' stickers on them were commonplace, particularly when the tough times of 1989 bit. Dad's business had its best year in 1988 – one of the few years that we actually dined at the local pub a few times – and Mum and Dad built a pool and put on a house extension. I'm sure they'd never have done either if they knew interest rates would soon hit 17 per cent.

Out of fear of further increases, Dad locked in the mortgage at a fixed rate of 19 per cent, and for the next couple of years we ate a lot of banana muffins – huge boxes of brown bananas were very cheap, and Mum was thrifty. We also ate a lot of those 'red spot special' sausages. My parents were stressed, and the mood was palpable. The private high school they'd applied to get me into was no longer an option.

We moan about rising interest rates today, but 17 per cent with no sign of reprieve felt far worse.

Pete looks back

I was born in Sheffield, England, and then later lived in Huddersfield, among other places. My dad's job was in probation and corrective services, and he had to move around a lot for work. There was high inflation at that time, and while my parents planned to buy their first home for £2000, by the time they were actually able to do it, they had to go out to distant suburbia and buy for £4000.

The world has changed a lot over the past four decades. There was no internet back then. Inflation and interest rates were much higher, and there wasn't anywhere near as much household wealth around. Cars were basic, most people didn't take out credit-card debt or invest in stocks and shares, and they had to save up to buy televisions and whitegoods.

When I was 13 years old, my parents told me we'd be moving again to another part of the country – Dad had to relocate for work. This meant a change of school for me, to a selective school requiring an entry exam.

High school isn't a great time to be losing friends and I wasn't remotely happy, though I tried to put on a brave face. Eventually, however, I found new friends, new interests, and ways to thrive in our shifting circumstances. That's just the way it is sometimes! Looking back now, I wouldn't change anything. Everything that happened has led me to where I am today.

Doubtless you've seen both the world and yourself change over your lifetime, as we have. Your goals and aspirations may well be quite different at the ages of 20, 40, and 60! And if you look back, it's likely that a lot has changed in in your life, career, and relationships in ways you weren't necessarily expecting. It's the same in investing. Stuff happens, and there's often not much you can do about it, apart from to keep moving forward and adjust course as you go – like a ship on a long voyage.

Adventure and investing

It's sometimes hard for Enneagram type 7s – 'Adventurers' – to envisage where and how they'll be living in the future. That doesn't mean they shouldn't make a long-term investment plan.

My wife and I have lived in Sydney, Darwin, Brisbane, and Noosa, as well as in East Timor and Europe. It would have been impossible to anticipate all of that; and, as with many couples, our life priorities changed dramatically when we had children. We just tweaked the details of our investing plan as needed and kept going.

So much of success in life comes down to perseverance.

Australia in 2050

What can we say about the future of property and property investing in Australia over the next few decades? We explored why property prices rise back in chapter 4 – remember, the key factors are a growing population, rising incomes and living standards, and a scarcity of land in areas in demand.

So, what will Australia look like in, say, 2050? At the time of writing, Australia's population is around 27 million; some projections have it increasing to almost 38 million by 2050. The population grows naturally by about half a per cent per annum due to there being more births than deaths, with the remainder of the population growth coming from immigration.

Essentially, Australia is a fairly high-population-growth country, and while it's not possible to make accurate predictions, Greater Sydney and Greater Melbourne will likely see an explosion in their respective populations towards 8 million over the next three decades, with Greater Brisbane also likely to experience dramatic growth.

Various locations within two hours of the major capital cities are slated for infrastructure investment, too, and will grow – these include Toowoomba, the Gold Coast, and the Sunshine Coast in Queensland; Newcastle, the Hunter Valley, the Central Coast, and Wollongong in New South Wales; and Bendigo, Ballarat, and Geelong in Victoria.

How will jobs change in the future? It's very difficult to predict. Technology is advancing faster than ever before, and the role of artificial intelligence (AI) and automation is potentially scary. AI and related technologies will probably bring both good and bad things to the world – like most changes! They will likely result in strong productivity gains for the economy over time, allowing the economy and wealth to grow faster. However, there could easily be an increase in wealth disparity, with the gains accruing to the advantage of the wealthiest sectors of the economy, creating a wider gap between the haves and the have-nots.

There's also a legitimate concern that AI could make many unskilled roles redundant. In fairness, though, we read articles 20 and 30 years ago saying similar things about new technologies then, and at the time of writing we have the lowest unemployment rate in more than 50 years! Those new technologies helped to create new roles in new industries, and there's no reason that can't continue to happen into the future, to some degree. Millions of Aussies will be employed in healthcare, higher education, science and technology, infrastructure, engineering, construction, government roles, and defence.

Where will people want to live? And what kind of properties will they want? School zones have become an increasingly important factor in determining where families want to live and buy property, and that's only going to be a growing trend over time as the population continues to increase. While we tend to think of ourselves as unique, we tend to be more alike as a population than we think. People tend to do fairly predictable things at fairly predictable times in their lives. Mostly, demand for housing will be focused in similar areas today: in the eight capital cities, and the peri-urban regional locations surrounding them.

Overall, we believe the cautious optimism that's one of the foundations of the Buy Right Approach is well founded. You can see that the key drivers of property price growth are likely – as far as they can be foreseen – to remain in play. Australia's population will gradually age over time, and although we may live for longer, on average, fertility rates will likely be lower too. Governments across many developed economies have become increasingly aware of demographic challenges over recent decades, hence the drive for strong immigration programs, especially in the younger and more skilled cohorts. As a result, the demand for land and housing in Australia is likely to remain very high over the long term, which means that property will continue to be a solid long-term investment.

Is there an argument that property prices in the future might grow at a slower rate than in the past? In short, yes. Back in 1993, Australia introduced an inflation target of 2 to 3 per cent per annum, and this has slowed and will continue to slow property price growth compared to previously – although, as we saw in chapter 4, the long-term property returns have remained very good.

On the other hand, the inflation target also means that the cost of living doesn't increase as rapidly as it used to. Yes, at the time of writing Australia is having cost-of-living issues, but anyone older than about 50 will think back with a shudder to those 17 per cent interest rates in the late 1980s and early 1990s and be thankful that it's not as bad as that, and likely won't be again.

We've had much lower average interest rates since the inflation target was set, as well, which means that mortgage debt – even now, with rates having risen significantly – is easier to service compared to the horrifying situation three decades ago. There will be market cycles, and challenges along the way, but the long-term outlook for Australia remains as bright as ever.

Reaping the benefits of change

Life and investing will always have ups and downs, but remember, change is often a good thing – for one thing, it means you're alive! Back in chapter 5, we explored why we feel that in property investing (as in life!) optimism wins, and how to combat negativity bias, leverage the positive influences in your life and build your self-belief and resilience.

Change is like a train pulling into a station: you can't prevent its arrival or halt it at the platform; you need to clamber aboard and move on to life's next stop. Champions embrace change and go with it, rather than continually trying to fight it.

You may have come across the Kübler-Ross model, first conceived in the 1960s, of the five stages of grief: denial, anger, bargaining, depression, and acceptance. Many changes involve a loss of sorts, and so variations on this model are often used by businesses to understand how their teams are coping with new projects or periods of disruption. The model can just as easily be applied to adverse changes in business or market conditions, the failure of an investment or a relationship, or the loss of a job or a key customer or contract. Our initial reaction to a change can be a refusal to acknowledge it (denial), followed by anger, and then a feeling of 'What's the point?'

The Kübler-Ross model isn't perfect – life isn't so linear and clear-cut – but it reminds us that the challenge is to move through the negativity, begin exploring and testing solutions, and ultimately accept the new reality and take positive action. Or, as we discussed in chapter 9, do absolutely nothing, if that turns out to be the best option!

If you do this, you can ultimately blossom and reap the benefits of the change.

Enjoy the journey

As we've said before, we see property investing as a way to buy back some of your time. If you can get quality assets compounding away for you, then you can take some of the focus off the need to earn more money and spend more of your time pursuing your passions and purpose.

Most importantly, try to enjoy the investing journey, even before you start to achieve time freedom. Otherwise, what's the point of it all? If you really dislike your job or what you do – and plenty of people experience this at various stages in their life – try to find a way to move towards something you're more passionate about.

Recalibrating your expectations and practicing gratitude are two other keys to happiness. In his book *The Happiness Curve: Why life gets better after 50*, Jonathan Rauch explains that relative happiness (or otherwise) can be driven by the gap between our expectations and reality. Did you know that people are generally happier after the age of 50? Life often gets better after 50, Rauch argues, partly because we learn to jump off the hedonic treadmill and be grateful for what we have. The dreaded mid-life crisis can thus be, in fact, a mid-life release!

Expecting everything to go right, whether in investing or in other aspects of your life, isn't realistic or useful. Most things worth having need to be earned, and comparing yourself to others may not help. Nobody gets every decision right, either, so try to be reasonable with yourself, as we've said before.

If you're naturally aspirational or ambitious, it can be tricky to strike a balance between striving for new goals and being thankful for what you've achieved to date. Be wary of setting a new target immediately after achieving an objective – take time to celebrate and be grateful for how far you've come.

Invest like a pro

Getting your priorities right, finding a career you love and maintaining a positive mindset are all important to the Buy Right Approach. What's our last, best tip on investing wisely in property?

Invest like a professional.

Take it seriously. You can do better than average, as we stated at the start of the book, precisely because most people in property markets don't even try to. Be systematic in your strategy, and keep records of your results. This is the only way to get real transparency on what's worked well versus what hasn't.

Then, as your portfolio grows beyond your ability to manage solo, do what professionals do and delegate! As we've touched on throughout the book, a great mortgage broker, buyer's agent, and property manager (for example) will be incredible assets. (If you find a terrific property manager, in particular, treat them as precious... because they are! The industry tends to be quite transient, with relatively low barriers to entry.)

Finally, keep reading, researching, and learning like a professional. The principles of successful property investing don't change all that much over time, but some of the specifics do, and there are always new trends and opportunities to be aware of.

As we've tried to show in this book, you can achieve truly great things over time if you understand some simple principles and action your Buy Right investment plan. The journey won't be smooth; there'll be ups and downs along the way. That's the way it is, and life would be boring if it was all completely predictable.

Now, it's over to you. Remember to enjoy the journey, and go for your life!

Key points in this chapter

- Australia is a high-population-growth country and is expected to continue to be over the next century.
- The world will inevitably change over time. You will change too, and that's fine!
- New technologies will accelerate the rate of change. Technology and AI will bring both threats and opportunities.
- There will be ups and downs along the way. Enjoy the journey! Otherwise, what's the point?

Appendix

Making property your profession

There are many ways to earn a good living from real estate. Most people know about real estate agents, but there are other professions within the industry, such as mortgage brokers, buyer's agents, property managers, builders, tradies, surveyors, and more.

Cate's journey to becoming a buyer's agent involved work in real estate sales and mortgage broking, which gave her an amazing industry overview.

Pete's journey into property as an author and buyer's agent came largely from his own experience as a property investor. He learned some things the hard way through his own investing journey, and then, as a buyer's agent, helped investors to avoid his mistakes.

Is a career in real estate for you? Only you can answer that. The benefits for us have included getting outside, meeting people, doing what we are passionate about and good at, and running our own businesses instead of having a boss telling us what to do all day. If you think a career in property may be of interest to you, seek out people who have tried real estate as a second career and sound them out for their experiences – good and bad.

What we do know is that in work, as in investing, if you can find an option that you're passionate about and you enjoy, you'll naturally do well at it and want to do it for longer. Since compound growth works best over the long term, this will put you at a tremendous advantage over your peers! As the great Jim Rohn said, success can be as simple as doing ordinary things extraordinarily well.

Glossary

Appreciation – the increase in value of a financial asset over time.

Capital gains tax (CGT) – a levy charged when an investment property is sold. At the time of writing, there is a discount available for investment properties owned for longer than 12 months, and no capital gains tax is charged on the sale of a principal place of residence. Rules are subject to change over time, however, so always check with your accountant.

Compound growth – a powerful investing concept whereby you earn returns on both your original investment *and* the returns you've received previously.

Depreciation – a decline in the value of an asset over time. Some investment properties qualify for deprecation benefits, meaning an on-paper tax deduction for the investor's annual tax return.

Enneagram – a model of the human psyche which attempts to categorise personality types.

Global financial crisis – sometimes known in Australia as the GFC. Refers to the severe economic meltdown of 2007 and 2008, precipitated by subprime lending in the USA.

Hockey stick growth – where growth plotted on a graph has a curve resembling an ice-hockey stick. In the early period on the graph, the flatter curve of the 'blade' represents a gradual improvement, but later the growth accelerates and curves more steeply, making the hockey stick shape.

Land-to-asset ratio – the ratio of the land value component of a property to the total value. For example, if a house is purchased for $500,000 and the value of the block of land is $250,000, then this represents a land-to-asset ratio of 50 per cent.

Lindy effect – a longevity theory that the longer a brand, non-perishable good, or technology has survived for, the longer it is likely to survive into the future.

Negative gearing – where the tax-deductible holding costs on a property exceed the rental income in a tax year, and the investor can reduce his or her taxable income by offsetting the net rental loss against other income.

Rent-vesting – a strategy involving renting where you live – which may prove to be cheaper from a monthly cashflow perspective – and investing in a portfolio of properties. All mortgage interest can be tax deductible in this scenario.

SMSF – self-managed superannuation fund. SMSFs are one method of saving for retirement, whereby the assets are managed by you. Normally, when property is purchased in a SMSF in Australia, it is purchased through a trust structure.

About the authors

Cate Bakos is the founder of **Cate Bakos Property**, a boutique independent Melbourne buyer's agency firm, and the winner of *Your Investment Property* magazine's Top Buyer's Agent of 2018 award. Cate was a finalist in 2013 and 2019 for the Telstra Business Woman of the Year, was the National Winner of the Buyer's Agent of the Year for Sterling Publishing in 2013, and a finalist for Industry Thought Leader of the Year and Buyer's Agent of Year in the Real Estate Business (REB) Awards 2019. Cate is President of the Real Estate Buyer's Agents' Association (REBAA) and a proud PIPA member, with QPIA (Qualified Property Investment Advisor) status.

Cate launched Cate Bakos Property in 2014 and has assisted more than 2000 clients with their property purchases, strategies, and decisions. Extensive asset-selection experience in Melbourne metro suburbs and Victorian regional markets has given her a valuable point of difference to offer her cashflow-driven clients.

She co-hosts the podcast *The Property Trio* (formerly *The Property Planner, Buyer and Professor*), bringing property topics to light and separating fact from fiction. She is also a regular media commentator, contributing to newspapers, live television, podcasts, publications, and commercial television. She shares her knowledge and experience regularly at seminars, volunteers her bidding skills often, and enjoys mentoring young people in the industry she loves.

At a personal level, Cate has continued to build a sizeable property portfolio alongside her husband and the pair have vast experience with renovating. Cate enjoys her spare time (especially

Sundays) with her husband and daughter in Yarraville's village and is a supporter of Melbourne's Inner West community.

Find out more at **catebakos.com.au**.

Pete Wargent is a finance and investment expert and the co-founder of **AllenWargent Property Buyers**, which has offices in Brisbane and Sydney. Pete trained as a chartered accountant in London and has worked for top accounting institutions and listed companies. He also holds a range of other financial qualifications, including diplomas in Financial Planning and Applied Corporate Governance, and is a Chartered Secretary.

Pete quit his full-time job at the age of 33, having achieved financial freedom through investing in shares, index funds, and investment properties. He is a keen blogger and posts his thoughts on finance, investment, the markets and more daily at petewargent.blogspot.com, which has over three million hits to date. Pete is co-host of *The Australian Property Podcast*, Australia's most trusted property podcast, and is the author of six previous books on personal finance, investing, and property. (Check out his full list of books in the 'Also by Pete and Cate' section.)

Find out more at **petewargent.com**.

Join our inner circle

We've been expert advisors to our clients for a combined 30 years.

Do you want an unfair advantage?

If so, why not apply to join our private mentoring group? Together, we mentor a small group of like-minded and ambitious individuals who want to achieve their goals through property.

Get in contact with us here and we'll let you know more about how you can join our inner circle and get the property insider's edge:

www.cateandpeteproperty.com.au

Also by Cate and Pete

By Cate Bakos

Successful Property Investment: 48 real-life property adventures and how you can benefit from them (Totalu, Melbourne, 2016)

By Pete Wargent

Get a Financial Grip: A simple plan for financial freedom (Big Sky Publishing, Sydney, 2012). Rated in the Top 10 Finance books of 2012 by Money magazine and Dymocks.

Four Green Houses and a Red Hotel: New strategies for creating wealth through property (Big Sky Publishing, Sydney, 2013)

Take a Financial Leap: The 3 golden rules for financial and life success (Big Sky Publishing, Sydney, 2015)

The Wealth Way: Unlock the power of compounding (Wilkinson Publishing, Melbourne 2017)

Wealth Ways for the Young: What the rich are teaching their kids about money today (Wilkinson Publishing, Melbourne, 2019)

Low Rates High Returns: Timeless investment principles the low-risk way with Stephen Moriarty (Wilkinson Publishing, Melbourne, 2020).

References

Chapter 2 – Who are you?

Covey, SR, *The 7 Habits of Highly Effective People*, Simon and Schuster, 1989.

Kagan, J, 'What is the 4% rule for withdrawals in retirement and how much can you spend?' *Investopedia*, updated 20 January 2022, investopedia.com/terms/f/four-percent-rule.asp.

Chapter 3 – What is the Buy Right Approach?

Housel, M, *The Psychology of Money: Timeless lessons on wealth, greed, and happiness*, Harriman House, 2020.

Taleb, NN, *Antifragile: Things that gain from disorder*, Random House, 2014.

Chapter 4 – Why property?

Koulizos, P, Are there indicators that can be used as predictive precursors to identify gentrification within an area?, thesis for Master of Urban and Regional Planning, University of Adelaide, October 2015.

Chapter 5 – Be cautiously optimistic

[no author], 'Record slump in house prices in 2011', *The Sydney Morning Herald*, 1 February 2012, smh.com.au/business/companies/record-slump-in-house-prices-in-2011-20120201-1qsid.html.

CoreLogic, 'Three years on from the pandemic: is the housing market going "back to normal"?' 13 March 2023, corelogic.com.au/news-research/news/2023/three-years-on-from-the-pandemic-is-the-housing-market-going-back-to-normal.

Kahneman, D, *Thinking, Fast and Slow*, Farar, Strous and Giroux, 2011.

Shorrocks, A, Davies, J, Lluberas, R & Waldenström, D, *Global Wealth Report 2023*, Credit Suisse AG, 15 June 2023, credit-suisse.com/about-us/en/reports-research/global-wealth-report.html.

Yeates, C, 'House prices could fall 32 per cent under "prolonged" slump: CBA', *The Sydney Morning Herald*, 13 May 2020, smh.com.au/business/banking-and-finance/house-prices-could-fall-32-per-cent-under-prolonged-slump-cba-20200513-p54sik.html.

Zhou, N, 'Australian house prices falling at fastest rate in a decade', *The Guardian*, 2 January 2019, theguardian.com/australia-news/2019/jan/02/australian-house-prices-falling-at-fastest-rate-in-a-decade-data-shows.

Chapter 6 – What can go wrong?

Levitin, D, 'What is the ideal age to retire? Never, according to a neuroscientist', 27 February 2020, ideas.ted.com/what-is-the-ideal-age-to-retire-never-according-to-a-neuroscientist/.

Lowe, J, *Damn Right! Behind the scenes with Berkshire Hathaway billionaire Charlie Munger*, Wiley, 2000.

Chapter 11 – Navigating the future

Rauch, J, *The Happiness Curve: Why life gets better after 50*, St. Martin's Press, 2018.

Australian Bureau of Statistics, 'Population Projections, Australia', 23 November 2023, abs.gov.au/statistics/people/population/population-projections-australia/2022-base-2071.

Be better with business books

MAJOR STREET

We hope you enjoy reading this book. We'd love you to post a review on social media or your favourite bookseller site. Please include the hashtag #majorstreetpublishing.

Major Street Publishing specialises in business, leadership, personal finance and motivational non-fiction books. If you'd like to receive regular updates about new Major Street books, email info@majorstreet.com.au and ask to be added to our mailing list.

Visit majorstreet.com.au to find out more about our books (print, audio and ebooks) and authors, read reviews and find links to our Your Next Read podcast.

We'd love you to follow us on social media.

in linkedin.com/company/major-street-publishing

f facebook.com/MajorStreetPublishing

📷 instagram.com/majorstreetpublishing

✖ @MajorStreetPub